CONTENTS

WELCOME

Right Rev Susan Brown
Moderator of the General Assembly of the Church of Scotland

Many people tend to see what happens on a Sunday morning or whenever a congregation meets for worship as the 'heart' of the Church's life. In many senses they would be right. As God's people, we are about gathering to worship God as the God who deserves all our worship.

But, our God, who is Father, Son and Holy Spirit, is also about community and relationship and as such sets an example for us to follow. Those who sit shoulder to shoulder to sing God's praises, to pray together and to listen to and for God's Word in worship are also, in God's name, meant to support one another, carry one another and care for one another.

All the way through the New Testament, Jesus' followers are encouraged to help each other through times of spiritual doubt, physical and mental sickness, grieving, hardship or suffering, as well as all the good times. Jesus himself reached out to those who needed very practical help as well as to those with physical and psychological needs. He noticed especially and made time for those whom others pushed aside and dismissed.

We are truly a community of God's people when we too care in that kind of holistic sense. We need to remember that God's love can be powerfully embodied in our spending time with a young mum stressed by the demands of a young family, in our drinking tea with someone who is elderly and housebound or in the time we make to listen to the person living with depression.

The reality is, however, that we worry about what to say, when to say it and how to say it. What if we should put our foot in it? What if we were to make matters worse? What if we said the wrong thing?

No one can guarantee that any of us will always get everything right in every situation. But, this publication offers a way for us to find the confidence to care enough to want to try. Let this book open the door for us to what it means to play an active part in being a family that cares – a family that cares for and about every aspect of the life of every individual in it – and that does so because . . .

That's what *God* does.

God cares.

Which is why we must. ■

WHAT AND WHY?

MY STORY

Doreen Eaglesham

Retired Teacher, Linlithgow

When my husband died four years ago after a year-long illness, I was devastated. During the first year, friends rallied round. But, as time goes on, they perceive you as 'getting better'. I learned to put on a public face, but inside was very different.

My status had changed. I no longer belonged to the same group of couples. I was included, but I felt I didn't belong. Friends would talk about what they were doing with their husbands and I felt completely isolated. If I tried to talk to my friends, they couldn't understand and I usually felt worse. So, I eventually stopped talking about my feelings. I didn't know anyone else who was in the same position as me to share what I was going through.

I had been going for one-to-one counselling and heard that the bereavement counselling team in St Michael's Church in Linlithgow was starting up a group for people who had lost their partners. I was really keen to go along and meet other people 'in the same boat'. At the first meeting, there were six there plus the leaders. We all shared our stories and after the meeting I left with a very heavy feeling. It was really hard to cope with others' grief on top of your own. However, as the weeks progressed we began to get to know each other and find support and encouragement from our shared experiences. How uplifting it was to hear someone else say, 'I KNOW what you are going through' or 'I have felt like that too'! I would come home with the reassurance that I was not alone.

For me the group was a lifeline. I found it helpful to talk and get my feelings out in the open and the group facilitated this. When new members joined and shared their stories, it enabled me to see that I had 'moved on' and that in itself was an encouragement. Others had been bereaved for longer and I could see the changes they had made in order to cope.

The group met for two years, which was a big commitment for the team of leaders, and over that time I formed some very strong friendships. We met socially to go for a meal or to the cinema as well as in the group setting. Although the group has formally ended, we still continue to meet regularly as friends. ■

Pastoral Care in the Bible

Alison Jack

Senior Lecturer in Bible and Literature and Assistant Principal of New College, University of Edinburgh

In the Scottish Metrical version of Psalm 100, dating back to 1564 and still found today in some hymnbooks, the psalmist asserts that 'We are God's flock, he doth us feed. And for his sheep he doth us take.'

The image of the people of God as a flock of sheep weaves its way through Scripture. 'The Lord is my Shepherd,' says the psalmist (Psalm 23.1). 'I am the Good Shepherd. I know my own,' says John's Jesus (John 10.14). A more 'pastoral' scene could scarcely be imagined as the basis of this image, even if the fields are far from the rolling hills and lush greenery, or even the craggy mountains, of our own land. Instead, think scrubby hillsides and plains, stepped terraces and extremes of cold and hot depending on the season and the time of day. But the genuine care and concern of the shepherd for the animals entrusted to him lies at the heart of the idea of pastoral care.

Another familiar biblical embodiment of pastoral care is, of course, the parable of the Good Samaritan (Luke 10). Those who walk by on the other side of the road to avoid the prone figure of the attacked man refuse to engage at any level with the person in trouble. In contrast, the Samaritan makes a connection, lifts the man onto his donkey, meets his immediate

needs and makes sure his future needs are covered too in the money he leaves with the innkeeper. He gets close enough to really see what the problem is and does what he can to help. He does not overwhelm the man, staying longer than is necessary or putting his own plans on hold to tend to him over an extended period. The encounter is brief, but the effect is transformative for the man left for dead.

The personal nature of the pastoral encounter in the parable is perhaps not so far from the perspective of the psalmist either. In fact, the use of 'flock' in the metrical psalm probably stems from a misunderstanding of an early English translation that used the Old English word for 'folk', *folck*. This was assumed to be a misprint for 'flock'. In most modern hymnbooks, the 'flock' of Psalm 100 as an image of the people of God has been nuanced slightly, at least in the first part of the line, to the much more accurate translation 'We are his *folk*, he doth us feed . . .' Folk have human faces, agency, opinions and needs that go beyond the physical ones of food, water and shelter more relevant to sheep. Perhaps as an image of pastoral care, 'folk' rather than 'flock' is a more appropriate image to describe the relationship between those in need and those with a desire to help. As a human reflection of a divine relationship of

> **Pastoral care may be understood as helping others to reach a new understanding of their life's narrative within the overarching story of God and his presence in the world.**

care and concern, it relates to the parable of the Good Samaritan in its presentation of personal engagement with those in need. Although the Samaritan, of course, would not have been considered as being of the same 'folk' as the Jewish man he rescues, at least in the perspective of some of Jesus' hearers.

The use of the Bible in practical theology and pastoral care in particular is not straightforward, and issues of the authority of Scripture and the appropriate application of biblical texts out of their original contexts are debated. However, it would be true to say that the parables of Jesus and the Psalms are among the most significant and most widely discussed areas of the Bible in the field of pastoral care.

The Psalms speak with confident conviction about the blessing of being God's folk, but they also offer a voice of lament to those who consider themselves powerless. Complaint, suffering and despair are given public and personal space in the worship of the people of God reflected in the Psalms. 'Why do you sleep, O Lord? Awake, do not cast us off for ever! Why do you hide your face? Why do you forget our affliction and oppression?' (Psalm 44.23–24). Allowing those voices to be heard and acknowledged, rather than suppressed or ignored, may be an important biblical witness and encouragement in pastoral care as it is offered and experienced.

The parables of Jesus offer a point of intersection between the narrative of people's lives and the story of God who is creator, redeemer and the one who sustains and rules but is also vulnerable and hidden. In their obliqueness they draw the reader or listener in; in their contradictions they raise questions about the meaning of an individual human life within a wider divine narrative. The parable of the Good Samaritan invites us to identify with different characters within the story: with those who walk past; with the one who is moved to help; and with the one who is helped. Parables such as this offer insights into the possibility of change and the significance of the one telling the story in the first place, who is the embodiment of the invisible God.

Pastoral care may be understood as helping others to reach a new understanding of their life's narrative within the overarching story of God and his presence in the world. The Bible in all its complexity may be a resource in that endeavour, but it also offers themes and perspectives that inform the practice, with Jesus as a paradigm. In Jesus' self-emptying incarnation, death and resurrection, as revealed in Scripture, we are given a model for our own reaching out to others. And we are offered the amazing possibility of encountering the living God in the stories we hear as a result. As Robert Anderson writes:

> The Bible is a resource of words that offers evocative images of hope and a transcending vision of God's relentless love that sustains as we care for one another in the darkness.[1] ∎

THINK

Reflect on the parable of the Good Samaritan. What does it suggest to you about Jesus' expectations about offering pastoral care to others and accepting it from others? Have you ever felt like the Samaritan, or the priest, or the man in the ditch?

What do the biblical images of being God's folk or flock imply in terms of caring for others and being cared for?

READ

Robert Anderson, 'The Bible and Pastoral Care', in Paul Ballard and Stephen R. Holmes, eds, *The Bible in Pastoral Practice: Readings in the Place and Function of Scripture in the Church* (London: Darton, Longman & Todd, 2005), 195–211.

Herbert Anderson and Edward Foley, *Mighty Stories, Dangerous Rituals* (San Francisco, CA: Jossey-Bass, 1998).

ACT

Be alert to times when you are tempted to cross the road to avoid interacting with someone in need. Ask yourself why that is and what you might do about it.

1   Robert Anderson, 'The Bible and Pastoral Care', in Paul Ballard and Stephen R. Holmes, eds, *The Bible in Pastoral Practice: Readings in the Place and Function of Scripture in the Church* (London: Darton, Longman & Todd, 2005), 210.

A Theology of Pastoral Care

Margaret Whipp

Lead Chaplain, Oxford University Hospitals

What do Christians mean by pastoral care? How might we faithfully follow the example of Christ the Good Shepherd in caring for other members of his flock (1 Peter 5.1–4)? A good theology of pastoral care helps us to think deeply about the importance of helping and healing others and how such practical concern bears witness to the life of Christ in our midst.

The shape of living

'The glory of God is a human person fully alive.' These inspiring words came from Irenaeus of Lyons, one of the second-century leaders of the Church, who stressed the fundamentally theological ground for Christian pastoral care. Whatever difficulties we face in life, we believe that the purpose of God is fulfilled in individual and collective human flourishing. This is central to the mission of Christ himself, who came that we should have *life in all its fullness* (John 10.10).

Christians believe that we are lovingly created in the image of God, who calls us into mutual relationship with his own goodness throughout all the changing scenes of life. This theological account of human nature underpins our vision of pastoral care, as we consider the shifting contours of human life and experience.

Life in all its times and seasons

Human beings come to birth, live and grow, flourish and struggle as creatures of time. Our mortal days are numbered, yet God has set eternity within our hearts (Ecclesiastes 3.11). And it is in the unfolding of our finite experience that God reaches out in love to touch and transfigure our lives. For this reason, pastoral care takes concern for every stage of life, from youth to old age, being sensitive to the unique opportunities for grace that arise at particular points of growth and transition, and not least in the face of the ultimate threshold of death.

Life in all its frustration and fragility

The vision of human flourishing, from a Christian perspective, does not deny the reality of suffering. On the contrary, we look to a Saviour who lived and died as a man of sorrows, acquainted with grief (Isaiah 53.3). Our faith recognises that it is often in the midst of the most challenging failure and frailty that human beings discover their greatest spiritual resources, finding, like St Paul, that God's strength is made perfect in human weakness (2 Corinthians 12.9).

Life in all its mutuality and communion

As members of God's Church, we need not face the joys and sorrows of life alone. We belong to one another in Christ, called to 'rejoice with those who rejoice, weep with those who weep' (Romans 12.15). This richly relational approach to life and human flourishing is rooted in our vision of the Trinitarian love of God, and it is deeply counter-cultural. When we truly bear one another's burdens, the watching world takes note: 'See how these Christians love one another!'

Life in all its hope and potential

A distinctively Christian perspective on pastoral care is the note of hope. Faced with the challenges and struggles of life, Christians are neither naïve nor despairing. We trust in the grace and guidance of God's Holy Spirit to work in us, and through us, for good. Even when we only glimpse the beginnings of healing and fulfilment, we hold onto a vision of a greater, heavenly glory that is yet to be revealed.

The glory of God is a human person fully alive.

A holistic approach to pastoral care integrates the best understandings of the human sciences with the deepest insights from an age-old tradition of spiritual direction.

The form of pastoral care

Learning to appreciate our human life and experience from a theological perspective helps to shape our priorities for pastoral care within the Church. It is fascinating to look back over the centuries of Church history to see how distinctive patterns of care reflected the challenges of changing times and social contexts. Many classic forms of pastoral care from earlier times can still inform and challenge our work today.

One of the great themes of New Testament writing is the **fellowship** (*koinonia* in Greek) of church communities. In a fearful and divided world, early Christians found their common bond in Christ to be a tremendous strength, as they urged one another to stand together in solidarity, love and mutual support. In our modern fragmented societies, where many suffer from loneliness and isolation, the caring hospitality of a healthy church community can be an invaluable lifeline both spiritually and practically.

The **cure of souls** (*cura animarum* in Latin) was a notable emphasis from the post-apostolic period onwards, as Christian teachers embraced a responsibility to guide the community forward, both morally and spiritually. This model of pastoral care reflects a therapeutic desire, like a good physician of the soul, to release God's people from their besetting sins. It also marked the beginnings of a more professional understanding of pastoral care, in which priests and leaders in each area studied to offer their best skills and learning in the oversight of the flock.

An element of **discipline** has always been essential for the integrity of Christian life and witness. Early Christian communities took seriously the boundaries of faithful witness, keen to preserve the purity of those who sought to walk the narrow road of Christian obedience. While scarcely fashionable in our own day, it is salutary to remember that in every age of renewal and reform a disciplined approach to spiritual and moral wellbeing has been crucial to the vitality of individuals and church communities.

The ministry of **counsel** takes many forms within pastoral care, as Christians seek to nourish and support one another in a deeper wisdom for life. Through individual guidance, as well as through the preaching and teaching of gathered worship, Christians down the ages have grappled together to seek the mind of Christ (1 Corinthians 2.16). Modern studies in psychology have sometimes separated secular counselling from its roots in spiritual guidance. A holistic approach to pastoral care integrates the best understandings of the human sciences with the deepest insights from an age-old tradition of spiritual direction.

A commitment to **liberation** remains an important radical aspect of Christian pastoral care, especially in situations of historic injustice and exclusion. Christians of every generation are called to stand up for the marginalised, and to work both personally and politically to challenge the unjust structures that perpetuate their oppressions. In more comfortable communities, it can be important to remember that an over-emphasis on individual pastoral care may disguise our quiet collusion with some serious and long-standing public injustices.

We can never 'copy and paste' our model of pastoral care from a different place or time to suit the particular needs of our contemporary community. We pray that the Holy Spirit will guide our caring and thinking for a greater vision of 'life in all its fullness' in our own day. ∎

THINK

Review the patterns of pastoral care described in the article – as fellowship, cure of souls, discipline, counsel and liberation. Which model seems to be most prevalent in your own experience of church life? Is there any emphasis that may be lacking?

READ

Margaret Whipp, *SCM Studyguide: Pastoral Theology* (London: SCM Press, 2013).

Robert C. Dykstra, *Images of Pastoral Care: Classic Readings* (St Louis, MO: Chalice Press, 2005).

ACT

Why not plan an evening with fellow church members to share Christian hospitality and discuss their ideas for a richer vision of pastoral care within (and beyond) the Church?

A Vision of Pastoral Care

Kenneth Jeffrey

Lecturer in Ministry Studies and Co-ordinator of the Centre for Ministry Studies, University of Aberdeen

In this article, I want to present a brief Christ-centred vision of pastoral care that is informed by our calling to become communities of priests, and that recognises the significance of small acts of kindness in the ordinary affairs of life.

'The Lord is my Shepherd'

In the Gospel of John, Jesus Christ said, 'I am the Good Shepherd' (John 10.11). This short proclamation defines the nature, character and ends of Christian pastoral care. It also provides a vision for our caring ministries. The Lord is our Shepherd. He is the faithful companion who leads and guides us, the generous host who cares and provides for us and the wounded healer who tends to our suffering, who keeps and sustains us. All our care finds its origin in Jesus Christ and in the gifts that he offers to the world. Pastoral care, then, is an invitation to all of us to participate in the mission of God by sharing with others the benefits of grace we receive from God.

'For God so loved the world . . .'

Agape love, sacrificial, self-giving and unconditioned love, is the greatest benefit of grace we receive from God through Jesus Christ. This is the love our crucified Saviour demonstrated when he died on the cross, the immeasurable love of God for the world. Receiving this love, by faith, enables us to claim our core, fundamental identity as the beloved children of God. It allows us to recognise that ultimately you and I are not the sum of what we do or don't do; we are not what other people say about us, nor are we the sum total of what we own or don't own. Rather, it allows us to acknowledge that we belong to God, that we are God's.[1] Pastoral care is about receiving God's love as a gift, accepting our identity as God's children and sharing this gift with others.[2] This requires a Holy Spirit-informed imagination that allows us to see ourselves and everyone else as the beloved of God and encourages us to become 'attentive to the presence of God in others'.[3]

'You will be for me a kingdom of priests'

Such a recognition of who we are together in the sight of God provides the opportunity for the creation of communities of care, where people can live and worship together at peace and with love for one another. When they were liberated from slavery, led across the Red Sea and gathered at Mount Sinai, the people of God received a new identity when they were told, 'You will be for me a kingdom of priests' (Exodus 19.6, NIV). Later, the apostle Peter described the early Christians as 'a chosen race, a royal priesthood, a holy nation, God's own people' (1 Peter 2.9). As communities of priests, they came to understand the responsibility they had been given towards each other. They were called to present each other before God and to present God to one another. In other words, they were invited to maintain a faithful relationship between themselves and God through praying for one another and by setting God's Word before one another. In this way, they acted as priests as they interceded on one another's behalf, blessed each other and kept God at the centre of their life together.[4] The 'one another' statements found scattered among the epistles (love one another; serve one another; bear one another's burdens; forgive one another; confess our sins to one another; instruct one another; comfort one another; encourage one another) reinforce the significance of this *koinonia*[5] kind of relationship the early Christians were called to foster among themselves. In a world today where old bonds and networks are dissolving, and at a time when more and more people are 'losing their tribes',[6] we are called to care for others by becoming a kingdom of priests and by committing ourselves to the creation and nurture of inclusive communities of belonging. We are invited to build safe places where, through our habits and practices, we share with one another the gift of God's love.[7]

1   Dietrich Bonhoeffer, 'Who am I?', poem from *Letters and Papers from Prison* (London: SCM Press, 1953), 173.

2   'Pastoral Care is, in essence, surprisingly simple. It has one fundamental aim: to help people to know love, both as something to be received and as something to give.' Alastair Campbell, *Paid to Care: The Limits of Professionalism in Pastoral Care* (London: SPCK, 1985), 1.

3   John Swinton, *Dementia: Living in the Memories of God* (Grand Rapids, MI: Eerdmans, 2012), 223.

4   John O'Donohue, *Benedictus: A Book of Blessings* (London: Bantam Press, 2007), 215–16.

5   Got Questions, 'What is koinonia?', www.gotquestions.org/koinonia.html (accessed 27 February 2018).

6   Simon Kuper, 'Loneliness is contributing to our increasingly tribal politics', *Financial Times*, 18 January 2018, www.ft.com/content/89f16688-fb15-11e7-a492-2c9be7f3120a (accessed 26 February 2018).

7   'The carer and the cared for are not on two sides of a divide which must be bridged by some form of expertise on the part of the one who cares. Pastoral care is grounded in mutuality, not in expertise . . . it is no more [and no less] than sharing with another in the experience of grace, a surprising, unsought gift.' Alastair Campbell, *Rediscovering Pastoral Care* (London: Darton, Longman & Todd, 1981), 15–16.

“ Pastoral care . . . is an invitation to all of us to participate in the mission of God

> **building communities of faith upon the practice of ordinary acts of kindness in the ordinary events of life among all people, everywhere**

'Take your everyday, ordinary life and place it before God as an offering'

These habits and practices include small acts of kindness that require us to pay attention to the ordinary, everyday events of daily life. Eugene Peterson insists that pastoral care is 'local . . . wholly specific and always personal'.[8] He encourages us to discern opportunities of caring in unexpected places in the ordinary events of life by slowing down and paying attention to the small things that surround us every day. It is, for most of us, the small, ordinary things of life that matter – the unexpected smile from a stranger in the street; the kind word of appreciation or encouragement; the unanticipated text message or phone call; five minutes of uninterrupted attention; somebody simply telling us we are loved; something that makes us happy and smile.[9] These small, simple acts of kindness only require that we become aware of the significance of paying attention to the little things of daily living and take the opportunity they present of caring for others. Jean Vanier, the founder of the L'Arche communities, once said, 'We are all called to do, not extraordinary things, but very ordinary things, with an extraordinary love that flows from the heart of God.'[10] On another occasion, he said: 'Love doesn't mean doing extraordinary or heroic things. It means knowing how to do ordinary things with tenderness.'[11]

This brief vision of pastoral care remains very simple. It is inspired by receiving and sharing the love of Jesus Christ. It involves accepting ourselves and recognising others as God's beloved. It invites us to participate in the mission of God by building communities of faith upon the practice of ordinary acts of kindness in the ordinary events of life among all people, everywhere. ■

8   Eugene H. Peterson, *Under the Unpredictable Plant: An Exploration in Vocational Holiness* (Grand Rapids, MI: Eerdmans, 1992), 117–48.
9   For a list of suggestions of small acts of kindness, see Paraclesis, www.paraclesis.org.uk (accessed 26 February 2018).
10 Jean Vanier, *Community and Growth* (Mahwah, NJ: Paulist Press, 1999), 298.
11 Vanier, *Community and Growth*, 220.

THINK

What helps/hinders you becoming more attentive to the presence of God in others?

What practices help foster inclusive communities of care?

What opportunities present themselves for you to offer small acts of kindness to others?

READ

Alastair Campbell, *Rediscovering Pastoral Care* (London: Darton, Longman & Todd, 1981).

Robert C. Dykstra, *Images of Pastoral Care: Classical Readings* (St Louis, MO: Chalice Press, 2005).

Eugene H. Peterson, *Five Smooth Stones for Pastoral Work* (Grand Rapids, MI: Eerdmans, 1992).

ACT

Text three people. Tell them you are glad they exist; it is good they are here.

Lord God,
your story is one of community and care.
From the beginning of creation
you have shown us ways in which
to offer comfort and consolation,
to protect and encourage,
to enter into one another's joys and sorrows,
to be human, knowing we are held
as, in love, we seek to hold others.

You have called us to make your story our own
in how we care for your people
in times of illness, distress and hopelessness.
Our only tools are our humanity
and the faith and trust you place in us.
Our only guideline is your commandment
to love one another.
Our only hope is that in the sharing of ourselves
others may be touched by your presence.

God of the widow, the orphan,
the refugee and the sick,
of the shunned, the strange,
the dirty and the dangerous,
help us to create new stories of caring
that reflect your yearning for all people
to know wholeness and healing
and that tell afresh of your presence
working through and within us.

Amen.

Tina Kemp, Associate Minister of Helensburgh Parish Church, Dumbarton

WHO AND WHERE?

MY STORY

Christopher C. Jones

Chair, Give-A-Kidney Scotland

When my wife Claire, without any prior symptoms, was diagnosed with secondary cancer, she was completely shattered with the news that any treatment may only slow down the inevitable spread of cancer. Our son – then thirty – was stoic but equally shocked, and my parents were totally devastated by the news. I took the news just as badly, but tried to stay focused and decided to 'stand strong'.

Being a carer never even entered my focus in any way. However, suddenly and without training or even street-savvy, I became a 'carer', not just for my wife, but it turned out effectively for my son, mother and father too! I had to take on a whole new role – the event planner, transport manager, family counsellor, barista, chef . . . It involved me in putting my own feelings to the side for most of the time, and merely 'putting on a brave face' for everyone else. I only had time to think about this 'new place' I found myself in during the late evenings when I was alone with my thoughts.

Caring, as I discovered, had many facets to it. The most obvious was the logistics of managing hospital visits, GPs, nurses, and so on while still running a household as normally as possible. The difficult part was in trying to ensure that Claire and I had enough time together – and with our son – to talk, reminisce and plan. This may sound easy but was hardly so. Frequent visits of friends and family, which at times led to clashes of visitors, often left Claire tired physically and mentally. I had to keep reminding myself that most importantly I had to keep the person I loved happy, secure, feeling loved and wanted.

Despite all of this, I found that period of caring for Claire immensely rewarding and fulfilling, feeling that I had genuinely made a difference to her end-of-life experience. It was a privilege to have been with her to the end and share that amazing journey that we will all take one day, and to have been her 'carer' for such a long period; it enabled us to connect and, I think, helped me to rationalise her death.

This unique experience has also brought my son and me closer together, as we shared that common bond of losing the most loved person in our life so much so that even now, after seven years, he still calls me at lunchtime to 'make sure that I am okay'! ∎

A Good Samaritan

Lezley Stewart

Recruitment and Support Secretary, Ministries Council of the Church of Scotland

There is a wonderful Scots word that I always associate with the parables of Jesus: the word is 'tapsalteerie'. The more common English form is 'topsy-turvy'. Many of the parables that Jesus tells are potentially transformative, because they turn understanding upside down and give an alternative and often surprising perspective. They offer a window onto a changed landscape when following Jesus' teaching and wisdom.

I remember as a child in Sunday school hearing the parable of the Good Samaritan (Luke 10.25–37) for the first time and being quite disgusted at the priest in the story! Although I didn't really understand much about Levites or Samaritans, I was pretty sure a priest was meant to be the one who would provide care for the man injured in the story. How could this priest just pass by and do nothing?

The question that initiates the telling of this parable is asked by a lawyer: 'Teacher, what must I do to inherit eternal life?' But it is Jesus' reply that offers the key to begin our considerations of pastoral care: 'You shall love the Lord your God with all your heart, and with all your soul, and with all your strength, and with all your mind; and your neighbour as yourself' (Luke 10.25–27).

The scene is set for an encounter that will offer an example of what it means to love God and neighbour and to offer pastoral care. The characters all take their place in the unfolding story: an unnamed man, robbers, a priest (religious leader), a Levite (a religious member of the tribe of Levi who often assisted priests in their temple duties), a Samaritan (considered to be of lower religious class and one who did not abide by the religious laws) and an innkeeper. Now, who offers care and compassion in this parable? Who is open to the needs of a stranger? Who gives support and hospitality? Who exhibits generosity?

Both the Samaritan and the innkeeper are the key responders in this story. While even the description of a 'good' Samaritan would have carried a shock value for Jesus' hearers, it is this Samaritan who sees someone in need and responds practically, pastorally and financially. He provides the care for the injured man at his point of need. The innkeeper also responds with welcome, a willingness to help and to trust that the Samaritan will fulfil his promise. Paradoxically, it is both the priest and the Levite who fail to respond to the need of a neighbour. By all accounts, most hearers of this parable would have expected it to be otherwise.

Often, we can fall into the same trap of thinking when it comes to the practice of pastoral care. We might consider that a minister or someone with particular specialised training is best placed to offer pastoral support and to identify how to respond to need. However, pastoral care does not have to be responding to a violent encounter with robbers, but simply the ability to see another and to respond with compassion and care for what they might be experiencing. While support from ministers or specially trained people should be expected for certain cases, there are many times when they would not necessarily be the best person to provide pastoral care, nor would they be the one to see the need first. Sometimes, it is the people closest in the community or congregation or in a particular social circle who can respond the most helpfully.

At times, we can be reticent in offering pastoral support to another if we feel we do not have the right skills or training. But, the Good Samaritan just offered what he could. He responded from the heart with a concern for someone who was hurting and bruised, and provided a caring and practical response. The best response is always one that is guided by the love of God and neighbour, a response of the heart, mind and soul: an expectation of the gifts another person can both offer and receive.

There are many occasions when it is doubtful whether anyone has the right words to say, and a ministry of presence and compassion is all that is needed. To be with someone in need, to share in their hurt and pain and to care is to respond to a neighbour in Christ's way. 'Go and do likewise,' says Jesus (Luke 10.37).

Sometimes, it is the people closest in the community or congregation or in a particular social circle who can respond the most helpfully.

There is an ancient Celtic prayer that encapsulates something of the mystery and majesty of responding to the need of another and signifies that it is in doing so that we can meet Christ in the stranger's guise:

> *I met a stranger yest'r e'een;*
> *I put food in the eating place,*
> *Drink in the drinking place,*
> *Music in the listening place;*
> *And, in the sacred name of the Triune,*
> *He blessed myself and my house,*
> *My cattle and my dear ones,*
> *And the lark said in her song,*
> *Often, often, often,*
> *Goes the Christ in the stranger's guise;*
> *Often, often, often,*
> *Goes the Christ in the stranger's guise.*

The call to care for another is part of the call of Christian discipleship to which all are invited to respond. To support another, and to pastor to another, is to find a way of living out that pastoral calling with compassion in its widest sense. What is key in the parable of the Good Samaritan, and key in the practice of pastoral care for all, is to know when a situation stretches beyond our own resources. Just as ministers will sometimes have to refer people needing support to other professional support services, such as counselling, it is a duty of care for all responding pastorally to know when a situation needs wider referral and support. Even in the parable, the Samaritan couldn't do everything and needed the innkeeper to provide a place and a space for healing.

Jesus' teaching offers a way of seeing things differently and the opportunity for us to consider again how we might each respond pastorally to the people and situations around us. ∎

THINK

Read the parable through and imagine yourself as the different characters in the story and what might be your natural response. How might you challenge yourself to see things differently?

Think about a situation where you wished you'd done more to support someone. What did you learn from that experience?

Think about a situation where you felt out of your depth in supporting someone. What did you learn from that experience that could lead to further development?

READ

Jill McGilvray, *God's Love in Action: Pastoral Care for Everyone* (Swindon: Acorn Press, 2016).

Henri Nouwen, *The Wounded Healer* (London: Darton, Longman & Todd, 2014).

David Benner, *The Gift of Being Yourself* (Downers Grove, IL: Inter-Varsity Press, 2015).

ACT

Consider what opportunities there might be in your own church and community to be involved in pastoral care.

Do other people identify pastoral skills in you? Could you benefit from support/ training to develop this further?

Caring Alongside Others

Mark R. Evans

Head of Spiritual Care, NHS Fife

Connections in context

In seeking to fulfil Christ's command to feed the hungry, care for the stranger and visit the sick (Matthew 25.34–40), the Church has sought to provide pastoral care that is both spiritual and practical. In the early Church, the sacred and the secular were interwoven and humanity looked to the Church to answer the age-old questions concerning life and death, illness and wellbeing. During the Enlightenment, the connection between the spiritual and the physical started to diverge. The Industrial Revolution led to increased social problems within the new cities. In response, there was a growth in charitable institutions while political moves sought to address social problems through the 'Reform Acts'.

During the twentieth century, the awareness of factors that contribute to wellbeing developed, as did the understanding of what individuals experiencing distress or uncertainty found helpful. At the same time, care professionals developed from being 'generalists' and became increasingly specialised. All this took place at a time when there had been a proliferation of 'self-help' groups aimed at supporting individuals. Such groups provide support for those with specific issues, concerns or conditions, for example Citizens Advice, Alcoholics Anonymous, Age Concern, CRUSE, SANDS and so on; the list is endless and ever increasing. There is a danger that such professionalisation and the increasing number of support groups may be seen as competing with, or eroding, the pastoral care traditionally offered by the Church. However, the reality is that rather than challenging the mission of the Church such developments offer boundless opportunities – opportunities for the Church to engage and work in partnership with others.

Connecting holistically

Human beings are far more than a mere collection of cells that need to be 'fixed' or 'analysed'. Wellbeing is far more than just physical health and true holistic care requires the physical, spiritual and social aspects of life to be cared for. Such a holistic understanding of wellbeing also requires a holistic approach to care. It is widely acknowledged that care is best provided when professionals and volunteers, agencies and communities work together with the person in need.

In the Gospels, those who came to Christ received a hospitable welcome as he journeyed with them in the search, offering acceptance, companionship and a listening ear. Alastair Campbell suggests that at the root of pastoral care is found 'companionship' and describes pastoral care as journeying with those in need, offering our support and love.[1] By walking with those in need, we offer 'intentional presence': companions on the road, listening to their fears, sharing their hopes and holding out the light of Christ in their darkness. By being present and by listening, pastoral carers can help individuals identify the help and support they need, thereby exploring possible sources of help.

Helping someone identify sources of help is referred to as 'signposting' and requires those providing pastoral care to have a good knowledge of sources of support including local and national agencies. Once we have 'signposted' the person to a source of support, our involvement should not stop. The delivery of pastoral care is not about 'doing' but rather about 'being'. It means being there for the person when the professionals have gone home, when the agencies have closed and when the person returns from an appointment with emotional wounds reopened. As such, caring for others is not a competition between professionals and volunteers or self-help group and Church. The best care is given when agencies work together for the benefit of the individual. And the Church has something unique to offer to such care.

 care is best provided when professionals and volunteers, agencies and communities work together with the person in need.

1   Alastair Campbell, *Rediscovering Pastoral Care*, 2nd edn (London: Darton, Longman & Todd, 1986), 87.

Developing connections

The Church of Scotland, with a presence in every part of Scotland, is ideally placed to support and contribute to the wellbeing of individuals and communities. Being at the heart of their community puts congregations in a prime position to initiate and coordinate projects and to work in partnership with others. Many professionals and agencies recognise the unique role of the Church and the care it can offer. As such, many agencies are willing to work in partnership with congregations to develop services that ensure individuals receive the most appropriate care. Such partnerships need to mean more than just providing a regular 'hall let'. It is about the Church creating a safe place, a welcoming place: a sanctuary to those in need.

The recent development of Dementia Cafes is an example of good partnership working between congregations and external agencies. The congregation provides a safe, welcoming venue and volunteers to organise activities and provide a listening ear. At the same time, staff and volunteers from external agencies, such as social work, community nurses, Alzheimer Scotland, are present to offer more specialised support. Such projects allow the pastoral and the practical, the secular and the sacred to become interwoven.

George MacLeod, the founder of the Iona Community, wrote:

> We must avoid the danger of . . . separateness . . . the tendency to concentrate on divine healing as if it can be an isolated recovery, sealed off from social concern. It comes, for instance, somewhere near blasphemy that we should merely pray for 'Margaret', suffering from TB (tuberculosis), when we know quite well this illness was contracted in a damp room in the slums of Glasgow.[2]

Connecting with ourselves

Working in partnership with other agencies requires us to have an awareness of our capabilities and, more importantly, our limitations. We need to ensure that the care we offer is appropriate and safe and that we know when, and how, to 'signpost' the person to specialised agencies or professionals. Many care professionals take time to reflect on the care they offer through supportive structures to ensure that care they provide is safe and appropriate. Within congregational settings, it is important that opportunities are developed to support those delivering pastoral care to reflect on and consider their work. Taking time to reflect on the care provided ensures that carers do not take on more than they are equipped to deal with, can identify training needs and know when to signpost to additional sources of help.

The Church has always cared for the sick, the bereaved and those struggling with life. Working in partnership with other agencies can allow the Church to develop and deliver creative and meaningful forms of pastoral care, where along with the physical and the social the spiritual needs of people are recognised, valued and met. It is only when we are open to working in partnership with others that we can support individuals and communities and enable them to (re)discover hope, meaning and purpose and truly follow Christ's command to 'feed the hungry, care for the stranger and visit the sick'. ∎

2 Ron Ferguson, *Daily Readings with George MacLeod* (Glasgow: Wild Goose Publications, 2009), 116.

THINK

Read the hymn: 'Servant Song' ('Brother, sister, let me serve you'), *Church Hymnary*, 4th edn (Norwich: Canterbury Press, 2005), 694.

What does it mean to travel with those in need as 'pilgrims on a journey'?

How can those we are called to serve help us?

Where do we find the 'Christ-light' in our own lives?

READ

Paul H. Ballard and John Pritchard, *Practical Theology in Action*, 2nd edn (London: SPCK, 2006).

David Lyall, *Integrity of Pastoral Care* (London: SPCK, 2001).

ACT

Ask members of the congregation about their knowledge and experience of local support groups and agencies. Arrange a meeting with locally based agencies and explore ways in which you could work in partnership.

In a Church Without Walls

Iain McFadzean

Chief Executive Officer, Work Place Chaplaincy Scotland

After speaking at a conference, I was asked, 'Is there a definitive text on workplace chaplaincy?' I replied, 'Yes! It is called the New Testament.'

There are many different expressions of chaplaincy. But all have, or should have, at their heart the expression of the love and compassion of the Gospel through sacrificial service, using actions as often, or more often, than words. Throughout his ministry, Christ was a servant. He sought to bring wholeness and life in all its fullness to all he encountered (John 10.10). To some this meant physical healing, while others needed to be fed, forgiven or simply accepted. His commandment to love our neighbour was illustrated in the story of the Good Samaritan, a story of action, service and sacrifice.

If pastoral care is a fundamental expression of our Christian faith rather than a speciality of a few professionals, where should this care be exercised? Again, questioned after a presentation on chaplaincy, 'You seem to be suggesting that we need to offer pastoral care wider than our church community. Surely we are not responsible for everyone?' I answered, 'No! Only those created in God's image.' If all were created in the image of God and Christ died for all, we seem to have a clearly defined mission field!

I have heard many definitions of chaplaincy; 'applied hingin aboot' was one of the most descriptive. But the most commonly used phrase to describe chaplaincy is 'a ministry of presence'. I personally find this to be one of the least helpful definitions. It is entirely possible to be present in any given situation and have no impact or effect whatsoever. Indeed, this is often the concern of many of our volunteer chaplains who say, 'I want to do something with my faith.'

The description of chaplaincy I prefer is 'a ministry of translation': the opportunity to translate the love and compassion of the Gospel into actions, and occasionally words, that can be understood and responded to by those we serve. The actions of Christ had an immediate impact not only on the recipient but on the witnesses too, whether this was the feeding of the hungry, the healing of the lame or the refusal to condemn those whom society and the establishment had already judged. Ordinary people saw in Christ something very different from the norm. Even those who fundamentally disagreed with Christ could not deny his actions. These actions led people to seek words of explanation, to want to know more and to re-examine their own lives and assumptions.

Chaplains are asked to start from the point of valuing all as created in God's image. This means that we must offer the same tolerance, acceptance, love and forgiveness to those outwith the Church as to those within. If, however, we do this simply as the prelude to convincing them that they are wrong and we are right, then we not only misunderstand the purpose of chaplaincy but we abuse the privilege of relationship and forget the humility inherent in our fallen nature.

> Surely we are not responsible for everyone?' . . . 'No! Only those created in God's image.'

Work Place Chaplaincy Scotland (WPCS), in one respect, fairly clearly describes what the organisation does. It provides chaplains to over 2,000 workplaces in Scotland. In another respect, however, the title does not explain the full width of the service provided. Would anyone dare to tell the mum with two toddlers that she is not working! Those caring for friends and relatives, those seeking employment and many others are often excluded from the generic description of 'workers'. For this reason, WPCS chaplains will often be found in situations apparently not covered by their descriptor. 'Listening posts' are regularly set up in shopping centres and busy thoroughfares. A few sofas, a coffee table, hot drinks and some well-trained individuals can be all it takes to convince people that they are valued, because someone will listen without judging, often signposting to other agencies who may be able to help, or (where appropriate) to local churches or other charities for ongoing support.

Wherever WPCS chaplains serve, whether fire station, shopping centre or Council office, their approach is always proactive. They will spend many hours visiting, chatting and more importantly listening to build up relationships of mutual trust and respect. Out of these relationships

we are called to be proactive, to offer sacrificial service in Christ's name

come the deep conversations of life and death, hope and hopelessness. These allow our chaplains to offer pastoral care (or pastoral support as it tends to be called in non-church settings), not as a tool to build churches or a strategy to raise funds but as an expression of Christian faith: a means to build the kingdom of God through actions as much as words.[1]

So, does it matter if pastoral care is exercised predominantly within church communities? Is it not enough that Christians are present in the world sustained by the teaching, nurturing and care they receive from their own worshipping community? Churches often respond generously when asked to fulfil a defined need, such as shelter for the homeless over winter or an appeal for disaster relief. 'If asked, we will respond.' Does this describe some churches' approach to pastoral support, and is that not a perfectly reasonable position? The answer, of course, is no! If the Good Samaritan had waited to be asked to help, the parable would have been

very different. The example of Christ was to offer actions before words, to spend time with the outcasts and sinners, to accept the unacceptable and to question the unquestionable. The care he offered was a direct result of the value he placed upon every human life. That value would lead Christ not only to exercise a servant ministry but ultimately to give his life for ALL people.

WPCS believes that we are called to be proactive, to offer sacrificial service in Christ's name in order that all created in the image of God might know that they are valued, accepted, loved and forgiven.

Pastoral care, or support, is not a tool to recruit people into the Church or indeed to keep them there. It is the fundamental expression of our Christian faith and witness, and as such must find expression well beyond the walls of our churches. ∎

1   For what pastoral care looks like, see Work Place Chaplaincy Scotland, 'How Chaplaincy Helped', www.wpcscotland.co.uk/index.php/benefits/how-chaplaincy-helped (accessed March 2018).

THINK

Where are the needs in your community and how might pastoral care be offered?

If we are called to care 'sacrificially', what does that mean for individual Christians and for churches?

What specifically might individuals and churches have to sacrifice in offering pastoral care beyond church walls?

READ

N. T. Wright, *The Day the Revolution Began: Reconsidering the Meaning of Jesus's Crucifixion* (San Francisco, CA: HarperOne, 2016).

Rick Rouse, *Beyond Church Walls: Cultivating a Culture of Care* (Minneapolis, MN: Fortress, 2016).

ACT

Consider listing the needs and challenges of the community around your church.

Read Luke 10.25–37 and ponder how you might 'go and do likewise' in your community.

What one thing could your church do today that would express the love of God to people outwith the Church, in a way they could understand and respond to?

Here I am, Lord.
Is it me, Lord?
Am I the one you want
to do the difficult job of loving
and of caring for your people?

Here I am, Lord.
Is it me, Lord?
The one who is called to stop and stoop
to lend a hand
when others would walk by?
The one who feels ill-equipped
to carry the weight of others on my shoulders?

Here I am, Lord.
It is me, Lord,
the one in whom you have paused to discover
something of worth and something worth sharing.
A hand reached out.
Arms to enfold.
Words of comfort.

Here I am, Lord.
It is me, Lord,
ready to share with others
the task of ministering to your people,
wherever you may lead.

Amen.

Tina Kemp, Associate Minister of Helensburgh Parish Church, Dumbarton

HOW?

MY STORY

Chris Leishman

Edinburgh

For fourteen years, I was a volunteer with the local branch of Samaritans (www.samaritans.org). This involved regular overnight duties, when the volunteers on duty slept on the premises and took calls from people experiencing all forms of distress: worry, depression, schizophrenia, suicidal feelings, family dilemmas and so on – you name it, we had it.

One night, I had a long and particularly distressing call. We had a debriefing system in the Samaritans, by which we were strongly encouraged to ring a group leader to 'offload' about calls if needed; but after the shift, I had a full working day, and then had to go on to an evening theology course. I didn't find a moment to make that call.

In the course of that evening, we were discussing liturgy and prayer. By half-time, I was struggling to hold back tears thinking about the call, and as soon as I could I took refuge in the toilets, where I spent the rest of the evening unable to stop crying. Afterwards, I was being given a lift home by a friend, whom I'll call Catherine. Without mentioning any details of the call, which of course were entirely confidential, I was able to talk through the feelings I'd been experiencing.

What contributed to my distress and why do I remember the evening so clearly? Of course, I was tired – little sleep, plus a full day's work – and after many years of Samaritan duties, that call remains in my memory as one of the saddest I ever took. I have no idea whether I helped the caller by being at the other end of the phone. She was too distressed to say. The question of 'Where is God in all this?' could hardly have been more acute.

I hadn't taken the chance to debrief in the normal way, but somehow the discussion of liturgy and prayer that evening had connected with it all, and helped to unlock my feelings. Catherine seemed to understand this. I remember little of what she said, but what has stayed with me very clearly was her unfussed, gentle, companionable listening.

My experience that evening reminded me that caring for each other is about ordinary people doing extraordinary things, and that it embodies an acceptance of our common humanity and vulnerability. The memory of this continues to influence me strongly in my pastoral work, and how we share and reflect on it. ∎

FUNDAMENTAL FEATURES OF CARING FOR OTHERS:

Pastoral Care as Being

Ewan Kelly
Associate Minister of Queen's Park Govanhill Parish Church, Glasgow

Pastoral care is essentially about being with. The carer seeks to establish a relationship that models the *agape* (unconditional love), acceptance and compassion of God. It is about journeying with another and not finding solutions or fixing problems for others. Pastoral care is person-centred. It begins where people are in life, not where we assume they are. It offers support to help others to respond to challenges in a manner appropriate to them as they seek meaning and resilience in their situation. As Alastair Campbell puts it, 'Pastoral care is surprisingly simple. It has one fundamental aim: to help people know love, both as something to be received and as something to give.'[1]

Self-awareness and intentional use of self

Pastoral care may be simple, yet paradoxically it is also complex,[2] because it involves human beings – both carer and the person(s) they journey with – in relationship.

The greatest resource a pastoral carer has to offer another is our self, our humanity – or rather, the self we are aware of, as we enter and as we are during a pastoral encounter. There are four areas to be self-aware about in caring for others.

Personal strengths or assets

Are you a person that others seek out for support or a listening ear? Are you genuinely interested in other people's stories? Can you listen without trying to solve other people's perceived problems? Can you listen without interrupting to share your comparative experiences or offer an opinion? If so, you are already offering sensitive pastoral care.

Henri Nouwen sums up the gifts required to offer sensitive pastoral care:

When we honestly ask ourselves which person in our lives means the most to us, we often find that it is those who, instead of giving advice, solutions, or cures, have chosen rather to share our pain . . . The friend who can be silent with us in a moment of despair or confusion, who can . . . tolerate not knowing, not curing, not healing and face with us the reality of our powerlessness, that is a friend who cares.[3]

Our wounds and vulnerabilities

Part of being human is to have experienced loss and transition. We carry the impact of those experiences with us into the pastoral relationships we make. None of us are complete or whole; all of us carry bruises or wounds. Rather than this being a negative thing, it can be a great asset. However, to what extent are we aware of these wounds and have we explored and accepted them as part of who we are? The concept of wounded healer is central to pastoral care:

The wounded healer heals because he or she is able to convey, as much by presence as by words used, both an awareness and transcendence of loss . . . Wounded healers heal because they, to some degree at least, have entered the depths of their own experience of loss and in those depths found hope again.[4]

A carer's role is not to fix or take away the pain but to accompany people through their hurt and confusion. Experience of loss is unique to any individual, yet personal knowledge of some kind of hurt by the carer can be a 'touching place'[5] or 'empathetic bridge'[6] between carer and the other. However, without awareness of our own wounds we can unconsciously seek to heal or ignore them by unintentionally interfering with the similar wounds of others and in doing so be a block to their and our own healing.[7] Thus, pastoral carers not only listen to stories, but carry or bear stories into a pastoral encounter.[8] Unless we are aware of the stories we bear and set them aside in the act of caring in order to make room to listen to the other, we cannot make a safe space for their story to be told, heard and explored as our stories will get in the way.

Limitations

Being aware of our limitations of time and energy are important prior to beginning a pastoral encounter. Both factors can inhibit our ability to listen and be present if we are internally 'clock-watching' or are unable to concentrate. Better perhaps to rearrange a meeting or call back another time rather than feel rushed or only partially present. Awareness too of our gender, age, culture and sexual orientation with respect to another is significant. Perhaps the person may feel limited in what they can

1   Alastair Campbell, *Rediscovering Pastoral Care*, 2nd edn (London: Darton, Longman & Todd, 1986), 1.

2   David Lyall, *Integrity of Pastoral Care* (London: SPCK, 2001).

3   Henri Nouwen, *Out of Solitude: Three Meditations on the Christian Life* (Notre Dame, IN: Ave Maria Press, 2004).

4   Campbell, *Rediscovering Pastoral Care*, 43.

5   John Bell and Graham Maule, 'Christ's is the World in which we Move', in *Church Hymnary*, 4th edn (Norwich: Canterbury Press, 2005), 724.

6   Stephen Muse, 'Keeping the Wellsprings of Ministry Clear', *Journal of Pastoral Care* 54, no. 3 (2000): 253–62.

7   Muse, 'Keeping the Wellsprings of Ministry Clear'.

8   Charles Gerkin, *An Introduction to Pastoral Care* (Nashville, TN: Abingdon Press, 1997).

> " The greatest resource a pastoral carer has to offer another is our self, our humanity.

A carer's role is not to fix or take away the pain but to accompany people through their hurt and confusion.

share with us due to differences in these aspects. However, it may be irrelevant. Avoiding assumptions and gently exploring if they would rather speak to another carer more appropriate, if available, may be helpful.

Power and caring

It is worth considering the issue of power in pastoral care. As carers, we may not feel very powerful, but as a person representing the Church we carry more power than we might think. For some, God is an all-powerful, judgemental being with the power over life and death. Illness or loss can be understood as God's punishment. This may well not be our understanding of God, but people's perceptions of God and how God relates to humanity vary greatly. The Church historically is an institution with the power to decide who to baptise, wed and where to bury. We are perceived as God's and the Church's representatives, and by association can be perceived to have power.

How we use power as a carer is significant. The very fact that the people we visit may be ill, infirm or upset means that they are vulnerable.[9] We need to be sensitive and enable such people to decline or shorten a visit should they wish. We will be entering their space: home, hospital bedside or room in a care home. We are their guest. Asking ourselves internally the question, 'Whose need is being met by my presence and how I am during or before a pastoral visit?' may help us monitor our use of power. ∎

THINK
Think of people who have journeyed with and supported you. What made their care helpful and significant?

How does your experience of loss and hurt inform the pastoral care you offer?

What does it mean to have power in a pastoral relationship (as a carer or a person being journeyed with)?

READ
Ewan Kelly, *Personhood and Presence: Self as a Resource for Spiritual and Pastoral Care* (London: T & T Clark, 2012).

Heather Smith and Mark Smith, *The Art of Helping Others: Being Around, Being There, Being Wise* (London: Jessica Kingsley, 2008).

ACT
Read Job 2.11–13 and John 11.28–37. How do you respond to these readings in terms of the pastoral care you may provide?

Keep a journal of your reflections on your pastoral encounters (making sure that those you care for are not identifiable) and ask yourself about each, 'What did that conversation/encounter say about me?'

9   For information on the Safeguarding Service and the Protecting Vulnerable Groups (PVG) Scheme, see www.churchofscotland.org.uk/about_us/safeguarding_service.

FUNDAMENTAL FEATURES OF CARING FOR OTHERS:

Pastoral Responses or Actions

Ewan Kelly
Associate Minister of Queen's Park Govanhill Parish Church, Glasgow

Listening

Part of the complexity of pastoral care is our attentiveness to the voices involved in any situation: the voice of the other(s), our spoken and internal voices as carers as well as the voice of the Holy Spirit. Listening, therefore, is not just done with our ears but our heart and our gut as we seek to discern when to be silent, to speak, to stay and to leave. Learning to trust our gut and risk going with what emerges from it can be a scary thing to do at first, and we will get it wrong from time to time. However, listening to our gut as well as learning from our past experiences can help us grow in practical wisdom. This involves picking up and responding to the feelings of others, which may be noticed in their body language and tone of voice. For example, 'I can hear (or see) how anxious that made you feel' or 'I notice how angry you are about that.' Reflection on our practice with trusted other(s), such as being part of a facilitated pastoral care group, is key to developing our pastoral practice, as is taking time to be still on our own and asking ourselves where God, or something of God, was while pondering over our pastoral encounters.

Certain listening skills can be used to encourage another to tell their story:

- Making eye contact during conversation, nodding and making appropriate encouraging sounds (such as 'uh-huh' or 'mmm') and facial gestures, while leaning forward conveys interest in and attentiveness to another when done in a relaxed natural way.
- Asking 'open' questions that encourage storytelling, which begin with 'How?' or 'What?', as opposed to 'closed' questions which people, if they choose, can respond to with 'yes' or 'no'. For example, 'How are you?' or 'How have you been doing since I last saw you?' rather than 'You must be sad,' 'Have you been out today?' or 'Has your daughter been round?'
- Reflecting back the last word or two of a sentence can help encourage another to tell their story. For example, 'I feel really lonely since my wife and I separated. I hadn't realised how much I would miss her being around. Even if we did bicker at least she was there.' Responding with, 'At least she was there . . .'
- Or enabling the storyteller to hear that we are listening and understand something of their predicament by reflecting back a key part of the story in our own words. Such as, 'You've felt isolated after your separation as it's only since then that you've realised how much of a companion your wife was.'

Speaking

In building up relationships and as pastoral relationships develop, the people we care for will very often want to hear something about our lives. They may not only want to 'suss us out' but also be genuinely interested in who we are. This is important in building trust and being open to receive as well as to give. However, if the focus of the relationship becomes about our need to be needed and cared for, we should talk this through with a trusted other such as a pastoral care team leader.

At the beginning of a pastoral visit to initiate conversation and to begin where people are rather than where we assume they are in life, it is helpful to ask an open question such as, 'How are you?' or 'How have you been?'

Prayer

Prayer can help meet people's spiritual needs and deepen pastoral engagement when it emerges out of a conversation within a relationship of trust.[1] However, it can also be a way of shutting down, ending and disrupting pastoral conversations when insensitively imposed. Whether or not to pray during pastoral encounters often provokes anxiety among pastoral carers. The key question as a carer is to ask ourselves, 'Whose need would be met by our saying a prayer?'

A few simple things to bear in mind include:

- Follow the clues regarding prayer within the person's storytelling. For example, they may be finding it hard to pray right now because of their situation. Offering to pray if they can't might be important.
- Ask at the end of the conversation, 'Is there anything I can do for you or would you like me to say a prayer before I go?', only if it feels comfortable/right for you and you sense for the other to do so. Again, you will not always get it right but through reflection you will grow in sensitivity and confidence.
- Keep it simple.
- Ask what the person might want prayed for.
- Use the names of significant people.
- Thank God for your time together and for the person you have visited.
- Don't be afraid to name the pastoral situation and the feelings evoked by it. For example, 'Loving God, thank you for John and the time we have spent together this evening. Be with him at this difficult and lonely time following his separation from Margaret. Help him to know

---

1 'Pray it Forward' cards, available at www.resourcingmission.org.uk/shop, can be of help for pastoral visits.

The key question as a carer is to ask ourselves, 'Whose need is being met?'

that you love him no matter what. In Jesus' name we pray, Amen.' Such prayers may evoke expression of feelings and tears as well as storytelling at a deeper level, as they affirm the person and God's love for them, whatever the situation, and acknowledge their hurt and pain. Such prayer only promotes healing following attentive presence and listening.

Endings
It is okay to say to people that you need to go. Overlong pastoral visits are draining and not helpful for either party. However, it is important that if you say you will go back for another visit that you do so, or find someone else appropriate to visit in your place. Telling folks as you leave that you will remember them in your prayers may be appreciated, again if it feels right for them and you to say so.

Referral
It is a good idea to talk to your pastoral team leader or minister if you feel that someone requires support that you are not able to give, and you should let the person you are supporting know you are doing so. If you have serious concerns, refer as soon as possible.

Doing
Pastoral care can also involve practical actions to support people at a time of need, depending on the gifts or assets of the carers concerned: for example, driving people to hospital appointments, doing the shopping for a housebound neighbour, delivering the church flowers or making a pot of soup or stew for a newly bereaved church member. ∎

THINK
Think about your gifts or assets in relation to pastoral care.

How do you begin and end pastoral visits?

What is the role of prayer in pastoral care?

READ
Christy Kenneally, *The New Curate* (Dublin: Mercier Press, 1997), especially Chapter 5.

Stewart Matthew and Ken Lawson, *Caring for God's People: A Handbook for Elders and Ministers on Pastoral Care*, 2nd edn (Edinburgh: Saint Andrew Press, 1995).

ACT
Plan regular evenings with those involved in offering pastoral care in your church to discuss and reflect on the care you offer. Ensure you have an experienced pastoral carer/facilitator to facilitate the discussion and help create a safe space for reflection to take place.

Take time to mull over a pastoral situation in a quiet space and ask yourself where God was, what of God was valued, in a particular encounter; let your mind wander in relation to biblical stories or themes, hymns, prayers or poems. How might what comes to mind inform your future care?

Participate in an active listening or counselling skills course (see local council or college/university evening classes).

FUNDAMENTAL FEATURES OF CARING FOR OTHERS:

Caring for the 'Self'

Gabrielle Dench

Pastoral Support Manager, Ministries Council of the Church of Scotland

'YOU CAN'T POUR FROM AN EMPTY CUP. TAKE CARE OF YOURSELF FIRST.'

As someone who is a huge advocate of pastoral care, its power and its importance as a ministry, I am also acutely aware of the importance and absolute imperative of caring for the self in order to be able to sustain effective, healthy, transformative and caring relationships with others.

The hazards of caring for others are not uncommon. 'Burnout' has become a term that describes the exhaustion that often comes for people committed to helping others. Burnout has been described as 'a state of fatigue or frustration brought about by devotion to a cause, way of life, or relationship that failed to produce the expected reward'.[1] In my role as Pastoral Support Manager, I am in a privileged position of meeting regularly with those who have a heart to be of service and to care for others. However, these same individuals often find it difficult to take care of themselves, and sadly symptoms of burnout are not uncommon.

Research in caring for the self suggests that many in caring professions feel that self-care is selfish. However, it is absolutely imperative that we challenge this belief. At the heart of pastoral care are personal relationships. In any caring relationship, good self-care will serve us in caring for others. Healthy caring relationships encompass the needs and limits of both the self and the other. When we don't care for ourselves, we can put others at risk.

Self-care strategies?

While it would be easy to offer simplistic formulas and advice, the reality is that often common-sense solutions do not work and even leave people feeling more frustrated and guilty. There are certainly no 'one size fits all' solutions to caring for the self. What I have found to be more effective is to encourage people who feel called to offer pastoral care to others to recognise three areas of the self: the physical, the emotional and the spiritual. A helpful discipline is to regularly take time to consider these three areas, recognising when you need to prioritise one or more of these aspects of your 'self'. Some people find it helpful to rank these major aspects of your wellbeing on a scale between one and ten. If you were to rate your physical, mental and spiritual life on a scale between one and ten right now, is there one that stands out as an initial area to prioritise?

Self-care tasks to consider

For those who find specific tasks helpful, here is a list of self-care tasks to consider:

Know yourself and your motivations for being a care-giver

It is not unhealthy to have your own needs and motivations when caring for others, which are part of us being human. What is unhealthy is not recognising or owning that we bring our own needs and motivations to any caring relationship. It can be difficult to manage these and keep them in a healthy space if we do not acknowledge that they are there.

---

1   Herbert J. Freudenberger and Geraldine Richelson, *Burn-Out: The High Cost of High Achievement* (Garden City, NY: Anchor Press, 1980), 13.

Understand your relational origins in family, religion and culture

These origins will have an impact on the way we offer care to others and the way we expect them to experience our care. It is important that we do not have the expectation that others will appreciate or even understand our approach to showing care and compassion for others. Some cultures are more reserved than others; for example, some have a harder time discussing vulnerabilities. It is important to recognise that you bring your own expectations based on your origins so that you can manage these in any care-giving encounter.

Invest in your intimate and primary relationships

Offering pastoral care to others can sometimes leave us feeling drained and emotionally stretched, especially when the care being offered is one-sided. It is important that you do not neglect the relationships in your life that are reciprocal and offer support to you. When we are busy or overwhelmed, it is often the most important relationships in our lives that we neglect.

Recognise appropriate support

It is important to know where you can go for support if you are finding a pastoral care situation difficult or if you just want to unpack a situation. Confidentiality should always be a priority so you may need to look outwith your immediate situation for confidential support/pastoral supervision.

Identify appropriate development opportunities

Recognise areas for personal and professional development that might enable you to care for yourself and others more effectively. Short courses in listening skills, retreat opportunities or even courses that encourage you in fresh spiritual disciplines can help you to care for your spiritual self.

Reflect on your pastoral care experiences

Take time to reflect on the good and the difficult. Recognise the aspects that felt challenging for you and those that felt positive. Reflecting is an important part of learning and developing as well as encouraging our own wellbeing by acknowledging the impact that any relational work has on it.

Healthy caring relationships encompass the needs and limits of both the self and the other. When we don't care for ourselves, we can put others at risk.

Balance work and recreation/seriousness and playfulness

If you have a difficult or draining pastoral care encounter, it is important that you allow yourself time to relax and switch off by doing something that you find relaxing or enjoyable afterwards. Sometimes it is easy to set aside a day for pastoral care visits or conversations. However, this is not always conducive to good caring for self and it may be better to spread these over a couple of days.

Attend to physical wellbeing

Looking after our bodies through exercise and a healthy diet is an important part of establishing and maintaining good wellbeing. When we are stressed or overwhelmed, we can easily neglect our physical health.

Attend to spiritual practices and theological reflection

When we are able to demonstrate the centrality and importance of our personal faith with those we are pastorally caring for, our lives can become a powerful testimony.

Acknowledge your limitations

Part of caring for someone well is recognising when they need more specialised support. Sometimes the most effective pastoral support you can offer is signposting to external support professionals. Other times simply listening or praying with someone is what is needed. Recognising the limitations of what you can offer is important not only in caring for the other but also in caring for yourself.

'An empty lantern provides no light. Self-care is the fuel that allows your light to shine brightly.' Unknown ∎

THINK

Can you think of a time when you said 'yes' when you should have said 'no'? What impact did this have on you?

Can you identify the people in your life who can offer you support as you care for others?

What development opportunities might help you to be more effective in your pastoral care ministry?

READ

Henri Nouwen, *The Wounded Healer* (London: Darton, Longman & Todd, 2014).

Margaret Zipse Kornfeld, *Cultivating Wholeness: A Guide to Care and Counselling in Faith Communities* (London: Continuum, 2000).

Kirk Byron Jones, *Rest in the Storm: Self-Care Strategies for Clergy and Other Caregivers* (Valley Forge, PA: Judson Press, 2001).

ACT

Why not take some time to give yourself a 'wellbeing assessment'? Think about the three different areas of your wellbeing: physical, emotional and spiritual. Can you rate these areas of wellbeing on a scale between one and ten? Is there an area that could be improved? If so, aim to come up with some specific goals to help you address this area, and share these with someone you trust so they can support you.

Comfort, O comfort my people.
You spoke those words long ago, Lord,
and yet they echo through the ages,
timeless and relevant,
a summons for today's disciples.

Lord God,
we take comfort through knowing
that in every aspect of life
you are loving and protecting us.
It is through the presence of your Spirit,
guiding, encouraging, consoling and inspiring,
that we are equipped to do the work
you ask us to do.

Yet we can be effective care-givers
only when we tend first to our own needs.
Remind us to be kind to ourselves
that we might be stronger for others.
Gently nudge us to a quiet place
when the work becomes too difficult.
Restore our spirits and refresh our souls,
make us ready again to serve your people.

Help us also to tread carefully
in our dealings with others:
to know the right time
to be silent or to speak,
to leave or to remain,
to seek help or to let it be,
to laugh or to cry,
to talk of future or of past.

Comfort, O comfort my people.
Assure us, Comforter God,
that you have gone before us,
are with us, and will remain after us,
in every situation we encounter.

Amen.

Tina Kemp, Associate Minister of Helensburgh Parish Church, Dumbarton

SELECTED THEMES

MY STORY

Kerry Reilly
Chief Executive Officer, YMCA Scotland

As a youth and community worker, building positive and trusting relationships with others built on equity and mutual respect has always been core to my work. In one of my past jobs, I worked closely with young mothers and their families. One young mum in particular comes to mind; for the purposes of this story, I will call her Heather.

Heather's partner had died and she was a single mum with five children, two of whom were autistic and one who suffered from severe anxiety. Heather herself also suffered from severe depression and sleep deprivation as a result of childhood trauma. She struggled to trust people and to form positive relationships with others. However, over time Heather and I built a positive relationship and she often liked to just meet for coffee and a chat. Heather craved adult company and I found that all she wanted was someone she could call a friend, someone she could share her concerns with and someone who wasn't going to judge her.

I didn't find providing pastoral support for Heather easy. It was difficult to understand and relate to her cycles of depression and personal struggles with her children. No matter how often I met her, or how much we talked, it didn't appear to have any impact on her mental health. I found it difficult to stay positive about our meetings. That was until I realised that my role wasn't to turn Heather's mental health around. I wasn't going to suddenly transform her into a positive, upbeat person; her mental health issues were severe and she needed professional counselling and support. My role was simply to be there to provide the adult company and friendship she needed.

As Christians, we often talk about the fact that we don't reap the harvest of the faith that we share with others. This can be just as true of pastoral care. We can't always see that we are making a difference. And that can be difficult. But, we have to believe that we are called to love others. That love, and care, can be as simple as building a positive and supportive relationship with an individual, providing friendship and a listening ear. It isn't always easy, but it is important. And it helps when we are able to recognise our personal limitations and the place of professional support alongside our role. ■

CARING FOR CHILDREN AND YOUNG PEOPLE:

Six 'I's

Gayle Taylor

Associate Minister for Children and Youth at Colinton Parish Church, Edinburgh

Having grown up in the Church and been in the ministry for nearly twenty years(!), I was and in some ways ironically still am considered to be a young person in the church. I would like to share six 'I's from my own pastoral care practice that I feel work well for children and young people.

Inclusion

I remember as a teenager, all four of my grandparents dying within two years. The minister and the elder visited the adults; children were not included. That experience has always shaped my practice of visiting a home. I always ask about the children. If it's a funeral visit, I ask if they will be coming to the service, and if not, how they will mark the ending and say their goodbye in a way that is appropriate for them.

Interest

Asking about children in a family is key to caring for the whole family. When I was a student minister, one of my supervisors always wrote down the names and ages of the children in the homes of each member. When he went back to visit, he knew how to follow up with what stage they were at and how they were getting on: going to school for the first time, playing in the school orchestra or football team, going up to high school or university, and so on. These things in family life are significant and the pastoral care approach here is being interested and acknowledging the joys. If we have cared about the whole family in the good times, they will be more likely to ask us to care for them in the bad and sad times. And, of course, it's not just the minister who can do this!

Insight

I remember from when I was a child the people who were kind to me and to other children in the church. In the days before safeguarding and training for Sunday school and youth leaders, it was hit and miss as to who would shout and boss you around and who would be genuine and caring. Tired school teachers who resented another day with children on a Sunday or bankers who liked to be in control were not the best people to ask to work with children in church!

The numbers at Sunday school in my day were huge; we were lumped together in groups randomly and I remember at one stage not having any friends in my group. I really didn't like going to church and felt the disconnection between the stories I was hearing about Jesus and the experience I was having. However, to this day I can recall one Bible class leader who spent time getting to know everyone in our group and who especially asked if I was okay when I'd missed a week. A youth leader who pays attention and has an insight into how difficult it can be to be a teenager or a child who is different, unhappy or left out of groups, is practising good pastoral care.

Involvement

In my current church, I love it when I see some of our older children beginning to help the younger ones without being told! The Sunday school staff have modelled how to be kind, caring and considerate. They have always asked the children to think about how others are feeling and to help them if they need anything. The other Sunday, a girl in primary seven noticed a wee girl of three feeling quite overwhelmed and worried as she didn't know how to join in a song. Very gently she tapped her on the shoulder and whispered something like, 'Come on and I'll show you.' The wee girl took her hand and went and stood beside her. Both of them were singing, doing actions and smiling within two minutes.

Incidents

In caring for children and young people, we need to visit the places where they are. Schools are crucially important. Youth organisations and groups and contact with their wider families are also essential. Children up to the age of sixteen, and for longer when we don't just look at the legalities, are dependent on the care of the adults in their lives. The big picture is needed in the pastoral care of young people even more so than with most adults, because things such as where they live, who looks after them, what resources they have and what's going on at home are largely outwith their choices and control.

When an 'incident' of ill health, behaviour, separation or loss happens in a young person's life, an understanding of their context helps us pay particular attention to what they need. Of course, we won't know every child who seeks us out or is sent to us. But, they will come to us because we know the school, their club or group or their family. They will feel that we are someone they can turn to.

Issues

There are many things that could be said about issues facing children and young people today and the particular aspects of pastoral care that could be applied in the Church. However, no child or young person needs the exact same care as another. All children and young people have emotional, physical, social and spatial needs, as do all adults. They are going through key stages of growing and developing and in this sense are extremely vulnerable.[1] The Church needs to be a safe space where young people can explore expressions of self, ask questions about life and find role models to help them navigate daily challenges. As well as having the safeguarding notices around our church, do we advertise and let young people and their families know how pastoral care is offered in our church?

Of course, some young people face challenges that are exceptional and extreme. Every member of the church can have empathy and concern for these young people. In these situations, however, a deeper level of pastoral care could be offered by those called, gifted, recognised and set apart for this role. Even those experienced and trained in the pastoral care of young people would need to work collaboratively with other individuals and organisations, such as psychologists, GPs, charities, social workers and schools. These partners have a wealth of resources to share.

Pastoral care for children and young people begins with the same principles as the pastoral care of all children of God no matter their age. It is rooted in relationship and made possible by layer upon layer of interest, empathy and respect. Jesus said, 'Let the little children come to me; do not stop them' (Mark 10.14). Once children and young people know (and they can sense it very quickly if you're not) that you are a person they can trust who is for them and on their side, you will not be able to stop them coming to you! ■

pastoral care for children and young people ... is rooted in relationship and made possible by layer upon layer of interest, empathy and respect.

THINK
With a group of elders or members of the congregation, think about your answers to the Year of Young People, Children and Young People Healthcheck (www.churchofscotland.org.uk/__data/assets/pdf_file/0007/46618/YOYP_Healthcheck.pdf).

READ
'Bishop Christopher's Call to Mission', www.southwark.anglican.org/downloads/FaithHopeLove/FHL2-Love.pdf (accessed May 2018).

Pastoral Care UK, 'Guidelines for Good Practice in Pastoral Care', www.pastoralcareuk.org/public/docs/pastoral-care/PCUK_Guidelines_for_Good_Practice_in_PC_Rev_20.09.pdf (accessed May 2018).

ACT
Design a pastoral care poster to go beside your safeguarding notices that will show young people that they and all their carers are welcomed in your church.

1   See the SHANARRI wheel (www.gov.scot/Topics/People/Young-People/gettingitright/wellbeing) for more information about the wellbeing of children and young people. All the wellbeing indicators in the wheel are necessary for a child or young person to reach their potential. They are used to record observations, events and concerns and as an aid to creating an individual plan for a child.

CARING FOR CHILDREN AND YOUNG PEOPLE:

In Times of Illness and Transition

Gayle Taylor

Associate Minister for Children and Youth at Colinton Parish Church, Edinburgh

Mental health awareness

Our awareness of mental health matters is crucial in all our pastoral care encounters, alongside our attention to spiritual and physical wellbeing. One of the most worthwhile things I have done in recent years is to have a wall display in the church cafe and a section in the Sunday service about Mental Health Awareness Week. Having the opportunity to find a way into conversations about how we all need to look after our mental health as well as our physical health, has enabled people to feel more confident and comfortable in sharing with us when they are struggling with depression and anxiety and other conditions. Opportunities in the school assembly programme to look at this are frequent, and in my own schools collaborative work with counselling in the guidance and pupil support department has been invaluable.

Transition and loss

Keeping an eye on and talking about ways of promoting good mental health particularly bears fruit in testing times of transition and loss. These times are frequent throughout childhood and adolescence as children move schools, change friends, have break-ups and find and lose their sense of identity (with all the self-esteem and body-image issues around this) as parents split up and when there is a bereavement. Seasons for Growth is a very effective group programme run in schools and in some churches and community settings that is worth exploring with young people.[1]

In times of a child's serious illness

If a child has been ill for a long time or has been diagnosed with a serious illness, keeping contact is crucial. The illness brings not only pain and discomfort but also isolation and restriction for the young person. The church contact can find ways confidentially and with the consent of the family to keep the family connected and to help the young person know that they are not forgotten. Telling a family and young person that we are remembering them in prayer is often a great comfort to them too.

Sensitivity to the young person's wishes is vital, as being ill often makes people feel a loss of control, dignity and privacy. Be guided by them, even more so than by their parents or carers, who don't always speak on behalf of their child. That being said, pastoral care of the whole family definitely

applies at this time. The church can offer care to the carers, who will need to be listened to and supported in practical ways. This can be a long journey with families, in that a consistent, thoughtful and sustainable approach is best, making sure that they and their experience are still welcomed within the church.

When a parent or carer is ill

If a child or young person has just learned that their parent or carer (it may be their grandparent who sometimes looks after them) is ill, they will be experiencing overwhelming feelings of worry and anxiety. Hearing their response to the news before getting into all the practicalities of what will happen next is vital. Some children may be visibly upset, while others may go very quiet. Noticing behaviour that is 'out of character' helps pastoral carers to monitor how someone is coping and to offer appropriate support. There will be lots of questions and how these are answered makes a big difference.

Many young people in our society today are young carers, looking after a parent and possibly also brothers and sisters at home. Relationships again will give us the context. But, what's important to remember is that the young people, no matter what responsibilities of circumstance they are having to deal with, still have the needs of a child – to be looked after and cared for themselves. Another good adult in their lives is a great gift: a confidante, someone who keeps an eye on their wellbeing and helps to give them a break from caring by offering practical support or time out. The Church has a good record in this regard.

Bereavement

Being part of the end of life of a family member or a friend is an overwhelming experience for children and young people. They need on-going and attentive support to explore their feelings and understand the impact of the bereavement in their lives. There are some general principles of how to care for and support a young person experiencing a bereavement:

- Remember that children grieve too, and it may not look like adult grief. Look for signs according to their age and stage of development.

---

1   For more information about Seasons for Growth, see www.seasonsforgrowth.org.uk.

“ children and young people ... need ongoing and attentive support to explore their feelings

- Protect children with the truth, not from it. Answer their questions; they are asking because they need to know. But, wait for them to ask; don't overload them with what you feel they should know.
- Remember that children are often very literal. Try not to use metaphors and phrases that may be more confusing later.
- Be guided by them (and their parents; check what they are saying and if they are okay with what you are saying). Children will often ask very deep and difficult questions one second and the next jump to something routine and ordinary. This is their way of letting you know that's as much as they can handle for now.
- Normalise how they feel. It's normal to feel sad, upset or sick when you're grieving.

Charities like Child Bereavement UK (CBUK) and Richmond's Hope provide support for children and young people facing bereavement. They also offer training to staff in hospitals, schools, hospices and other institutions throughout the UK as well as support for staff and families who have experienced a bereavement.

When it is the child who is dying – and sadly this is a situation that more families than we realise go through – hospital chaplains and the Children's Hospices Across Scotland (CHAS) give wonderful, gracious and selfless care to young people going through this. There are a number of excellent charities and organisations (see below) very willing to help families, groups and communities in knowing what they can do to offer care too. ■

THINK
Think about the SHANARRI wheel[2] and how your church is attending to these areas of wellbeing for children and young people.

READ
Eliza Jane Baker, 'How Do We Assess and Meet the Spiritual Needs of Young People in Hospital?', www.stjohns-nottm.ac.uk/assets/Website-pdf-files-2015/Chaplaincy/Student-Essays/How-do-we-assess-and-meet-spiritual-needs-of-young-people-in-hospital..pdf (accessed May 2018).

ACT
Why not invite speakers to your Kirk session or children and youth subgroup from charities and organisations offering resources and support? For example, CBUK, Cancer and Leukaemia in Childhood (CLIC) Sargent, Richmond's Hope, Place2Be, CHAS, Child and Adolescent Mental Health Services (CAMHS), Barnardo's, Children 1st.

RELATIONSHIPS AND SEPARATION:

Relationships

Blair Robertson

Senior Pastoral Supervisor with the Association of Pastoral Supervisors and Educators (APSE)

To get you thinking

Before you begin to read this article, take a moment to consider the various types of relationships that are present in your family, among your friends and in the congregation. Make a list of them all.

It might include marriage, co-habitation, divorced, separated or remarried. You may know or be aware of people in a same-sex marriage or a civil partnership. And within the variety of relationships, those who are widowed must be included, for a relationship with a deceased person continues though in a different form, and it can sometimes be difficult for the bereaved to form new intimate relationships.

When you have written a list of all the types of relationships you know people are in, have a slow read through it and become aware of how you are reacting and any questions that arise for you. Do this without judgement or criticism. You might be surprised to realise that you know so many divorced or separated people or that you are unaware of anyone in a same-sex relationship. You may also like to reflect on how social attitudes to the variety of human relationships have changed within your own lifetime.

Relationships are important

The relationships we are in, as spouses, friends, parents or whatever, are deeply important to us, particularly those we choose to form and which become intimate and committed. In considering such relationships, we are walking on holy ground. Recall the instruction God gave to Moses when he stood at the burning bush: 'Remove the sandals from your feet, for the place on which you are standing is holy ground' (Exodus 3.5). Shoes are removed as a sign of respect to avoid damaging the sacred ground and as a first step towards empathy (we remove our shoes so that it might be possible to imagine wearing the shoes of other people!). Human relationships are sacred and holy to those who are in them. We can never afford to treat the relationships people are in lightly or casually. As an example of this, consider the care that parents of teenagers must exercise when the teenager begins to bring home their boyfriends or girlfriends hoping for parental approval!

Further, the deepest and most important relationships people have are often mysterious to those on the outside looking in – and even also to those who are in the relationship. We can never fully understand why we fall in love with the person we do, and often we can't understand why our friends' marriages endure and flourish. Human relationships are often a mystery to those who look on as observers. So, the teaching of Jesus not to judge (Matthew 7.1–5) is worth holding in mind. It is possible, however, to understand something of our motivations and behaviours through psychology or counselling.

Relationships are important because they are a crucial part of what it means to be a human being; humans are social creatures made for relationships. And we flourish as humans when we exist within supportive, loving and nurturing relationships. In the story of the creation of humankind, God declares that 'It is not good that the man should be alone' (Genesis 2.18). Psychological, emotional, sexual and intellectual needs can be met in our relationships. We will all have seen how some people flourish because of the relationships they have in their place of work and how others become withdrawn and bitter as a result of criticism or indifference in their homes. Relationships are important for growth in emotional wellbeing, self-awareness and self-respect. This is most significantly true of marriage or other committed, intimate relationships; they can be like an incubator in which people grow as individuals and as a couple – as 'one flesh' – and the fruits of grace, patience and love flourish.

we flourish as humans when we exist within supportive, loving and nurturing relationships.

The Church and human relationships

As a result of this, it is not surprising that the Church has had an interest in human relationships from the beginning; the love Christians have for each other is a sign that they are Christ's disciples (John 13.35). The bond of marriage is to be a reflection of the bond of Christ and the Church (e.g. Ephesians 5). The teaching of the Church on human relationships has changed throughout history and across cultures and denominations. At one time, people who had divorced were not accepted in the Church, because marriage was regarded as a sacred and unbreakable bond; the current debate in the Church revolves around the acceptability of same-sex marriage. The teaching of the Church on marriage centres on the ethics of sex and sexuality: what is permissible and what is not. The views of society have changed remarkably in recent years and the Church has struggled to know how to accommodate or resist these changes.

One way in which the Church has affirmed people in their relationships is through its worship and liturgy. People were getting married before the Church got involved. But many people still look to the Church to help them to celebrate a marriage, to thank God for their relationship and to seek the blessing of God on their love. In recent years, non-religious weddings have become more popular, often conducted by the Humanist Society or simply by the registrar. The need for a ritual, or a rite of passage, that is shared with family and friends (in effect a ceremony that gives social sanction to a personal and private matter) would seem to be a deeply human need. The Church is also often asked to give a blessing to a civil marriage or to facilitate the renewal or reaffirmation of the vows of marriage. The Church of Scotland's Book of Common Order contains services for all of these. They are important opportunities for the Church to speak out what it believes about the nature of human relationships and about the God who is the source and strength of love, and to embody in pastoral concern the compassion and hope of God. ■

THINK

Look back in your life and recall people whose relationships you admired; perhaps a couple who were together for many, many years or a family who endured through adversity. What are the qualities of their relationships that you admire and would give thanks to God for?

A young woman and a young man sat in the study of the manse speaking with the minister about their marriage plans. After a while, the young man hesitatingly said to the minister, 'I suppose we should tell you that we're living in sin.' The minister gently smiled and said, 'I'd hope you were living in love. But, how's it going?' The young couple seemed a bit surprised at this response . . . and relieved!

What do you make of the response?

READ

Jessica Rose, *Psychology for Pastoral Contexts* (London: SCM Press, 2013), especially Part 2, 'Some Building Blocks in Psychology', for an understanding of the psychology underlying our relationships.

David G. Myers and Letha Dawson Scanzoni, *What God Has Joined Together* (New York: HarperCollins, 2005), for an exploration of the benefits of marriage to individuals and society, leading to a Christian argument for same-sex marriage, a contested contemporary topic.

ACT

Consider what your congregation does to support people planning to get married or the newly married. Explore how your congregation could support those not married but in committed relationships. Why not arrange an information evening hosted by the congregation covering matters such as wills, financial planning and communication in a relationship.

RELATIONSHIPS AND SEPARATION:

Separation

Blair Robertson

Senior Pastoral Supervisor with the Association of Pastoral Supervisors and Educators (APSE)

Relationships have beginnings – and sometimes endings too

Despite the significance of human relationships and the desire of society and the Church to support people in their loves and their lives, it is a reality that relationships are not easy and often break down. To say that it is a sadness when married couples divorce is not to make a judgement but to acknowledge the emotional distress and pain that comes with divorce and which may have been present for some time within the marriage. Separation and divorce cause hurt and disappointment for all involved – families, friends and the church community; an appropriate pastoral response will be compassionate and non-judgemental. Generally, people will be feeling distressed and 'down' when a relationship comes to an end. So, it is not the task of pastoral care to compound these feelings by clumsy care!

To continue the metaphor of holy ground from earlier, we might say that the end of a relationship is like an earthquake, shattering the ground into pieces, leaving all who were standing on it shaken and searching for safety.

Relationships can come under stress and end for a number of reasons, but the common factors are change and communication; the couple, individually or together, go through a significant change, creating an experiential and emotional distance between them. They become unable, for whatever reason, to communicate across this gap. The changes may be about finance, illness or injury, employment or sexual difficulties. It is also recognised that the loss of a child, or the inability to have a child, can be a hugely significant cause of stress in a relationship.

The needs of children

When parents decide to separate and then divorce, the needs of their children are worthy of the pastoral concern of the congregation. While children and teenagers will not be unfamiliar with the idea of parents separating (they will likely have friends at school whose parents are no longer together), the fact that it is happening to them will probably be distressing and bewildering. It is likely that they will blame themselves in some way for what their parents are doing, and experience emotions that they can't understand or easily talk about. Children and teenagers, therefore, need reassurance that they are not the cause of their parents' relationship ending. Blame can also lead to shame, and young people need to know that they are of value to their friends, to the Church and to God. The emotions they are experiencing may lead them to behave in uncharacteristic ways – 'acting out' – and adults working with these young people need to exercise patience and wisdom. Importantly, at a time of change and confusion, adults in the congregation who work with young people can be a reliable, trustworthy and dependable adult presence.

Pastoral care and endings

The end of a relationship is a form of loss, and the familiar emotional landscape of grief is just as relevant here as with a death: shock and disbelief, anger and guilt, sadness and readjustment. As with all aspects of pastoral care, some basic principles are worth bearing in mind when working with adults and young people who are in the midst of a relationship breakdown:

- Be accepting of what is happening and try to avoid passing judgements; you will not know the whole story.
- Be accepting of the emotions people are experiencing and try not to tell people what they should or should not be feeling.
- Try not to take sides; be neutral, remembering that human relationships are often complex and especially so when they go wrong.
- Remember that much of normal life goes on. It can be very important for young people especially to be supported to continue with their usual activities, such as their own organisations in the church.
- Be aware of your own feelings and opinions and try to 'bracket them off' as best you can.

> " **an appropriate pastoral response will be compassionate and non-judgemental.**

What can the Church do?

As the Church is involved in helping people to celebrate the beginnings of committed relationships, we might wonder what it could or ought to do to help people negotiate the end of a relationship. It is often the case, however, that couples who are divorcing stop attending church perhaps due to a sense of failure and shame. Some Christian churches, because of their particular theological understanding of marriage, are less accepting of divorce, for example, and it can be difficult for divorced people to participate fully in their life and worship. Nevertheless, Christian concepts such as forgiveness, repentance, hope and resurrection are relevant to the endings of relationships. Sensitive preaching and pastoral care will wish to weave these into the lives that people are living. For example, when divorced people are marrying new partners, it might be possible for the marriage service to speak words of truth about the past but also words of hope, trust and new beginnings. Furthermore, what might a Christian ritual for the ending of a relationship be like? It is important that the theology and worship of the Church engages with the reality of people's lives and not just the happy or easy bits. ■

THINK

Do you know anyone who has gone through separation and perhaps also a divorce? What might you learn from their experience? If you feel able, ask to have a conversation with them and to ask three questions: What helped you at the time? What did not help you? What was missing that could have helped? This is a listening exercise for you and a thinking exercise for both of you.

I recently learned that friends – two couples – were separating. After the initial surprise and sadness, there was the question of how I was going to respond. I chose to contact each person individually, by letter or e-mail, to give the same assurance of ongoing friendship, love and welcome. While I was aware of the question, 'I wonder what happened?' being asked inside myself, I knew that I did not know, did not need to know and probably will never know the story that resulted in the ending of those relationships. And maybe even the people involved don't really know or understand either.

Have you been in a similar situation?

What did you do? What did you not do?

How did you feel?

READ

Relationships Scotland (www.relationships-scotland. org.uk) for information about relationships, and the resources and help offered.

Citizens Advice Scotland (www.citizensadvice. org.uk/scotland/family) for information about getting married, legal aspects of different types of relationships and ending relationships. It's worth noting that the law in Scotland pertaining to marriage and divorce is different from the rest of the UK.

ACT

Do some research and compile a list of organisations and agencies in your area that give help to couples and families when relationships are going wrong. It might include Relationships Scotland, Women's Aid, Citizens Advice and Family Counselling services.

Different stages in a person's lifetime can have different loneliness triggers.

LONELINESS AND ISOLATION:

Stay Here and Keep Watch with Me

Janet P. Foggie

Pioneer Minister, Church of Scotland Chaplain to the University of Stirling

Feeling lonely

Being alone is one of the fundamental experiences of every human. Jesus chose to be alone in the wilderness before his ministry began, where he was tested by the devil. Several times in the Gospels he also chose to be alone when a large crowd followed him. His choice to be alone at his lowest ebb in Gethsemane was a desire to plead with God without being overheard; yet he did need his friends to watch and pray. 'Stay here and keep watch with me' (Matthew 26.38, NIV), he asked them. It was a request they did not manage to fulfil.

In the literature on loneliness and isolation, sometimes termed 'social isolation', loneliness is always seen in a negative light. The choice to be alone for spiritual growth or in order to pray undisturbed is not covered in the literature, nor is the 'blissful solitude' Wordsworth speaks of in his poem 'Daffodils'. The loneliness that is considered here is about when the person who desperately needs company is let down by friends or society at large, as in that moment when Jesus woke his disciples three times in Matthew 26.36–46 and yet they were unable to sit awake near him or with him as he needed.

One point upon which all the literature agrees is that loneliness is a feeling. It is the perception of an individual who feels disconnected or alone. This feeling may relate to a set of specific circumstances; for Jesus, it was the moment his best friends fell asleep when their company was truly needed. For any person, it could be a bereavement, a divorce or a house move. But it can also be a feeling that is unique to the person feeling lonely.

The age factor

Different stages in a person's lifetime can have different loneliness triggers. The loneliness of the teenager or young adult may be due to rural isolation or isolation through poverty, or it may be a feeling of not yet having found one's niche. Comparisons or communications with other young adults may seem easy to make on social media and yet these contacts may not prevent the individual from feeling lonely. For students, moving away from home may contribute to feelings of loneliness.

New parents also often experience loneliness as their ability to socialise is affected and the experience of becoming a parent may separate them from former friend groups. Another research paper suggested that the forty-five to fifty-four age group was the most likely to self-identify as lonely and the group that was most likely to socialise or see friends less than once a week.[1]

There is a fair amount of research on the loneliness felt by older people in their own homes or in nursing home placements where their social needs are not met. Those needing only personal care can feel very alone in a nursing home where the predominant population suffers from some form of dementia, for example. This person is not isolated in absolute terms but is lonely because the other people around them cannot meet their social needs. People who are socially isolated are more likely to have more complex health stories with less support available if they are diagnosed with cancer or Alzheimer's disease.[2]

Pastoral care to older people needs to be sensitive to the possibility that the older person may be feeling loneliness as a result of isolation. But, it is important not to make an initial assumption that this is the case. Some older people are very well connected and continue to provide support, emotional and social, for younger people in their communities or families. As a parish minister, I provided pastoral care to a woman in her eighties who had lived with a diagnosis of multiple sclerosis (MS) since her forties. Although she was bedridden for fifteen years before her death, she had a huge range of people in and out of her house and a loving family. At her funeral, the people who came to celebrate and remember her life spoke of what she did for them rather than what they did for her. She had been severely disabled by her illness, but she was neither socially isolated nor lonely.

Loneliness and loss

The loneliness of bereavement is a very specific loneliness. A person who has a busy and active social life, a happy family and a good job, can still feel deeply lonely as a result of bereavement. The loss of a specific person who is loved by us or close to us may lead to a feeling of loneliness for that irreplaceable individual. Other losses can be similarly specific; following a house fire or burglary, the loss of personal items and familiar things can bring back significant grieving for persons long dead. Or after a move or upheaval, the loss of sharing that new experience with our deceased

1   Hardeep Aiden, *Isolation and Loneliness: An Overview of the Literature* (London: British Red Cross, 2016), www.redcross.org.uk/about-us/what-we-do/research-publications.
2   Voluntary Health Scotland, 'Loneliness: A Threat to Scotland's Health', briefing paper, www.vhscotland.org.uk/wp-content/uploads/2017/03/Loneliness-Briefing-Paper.pdf (accessed January 2018).

loved one can lead to piercing feelings of loneliness that the person feeling them may find difficult to put into words. For individuals who have moved country within their lifetime and especially refugees, complex losses of place, of people and also of personal identities may lead to a compounded feeling of loneliness exacerbated by cultural and social isolation at times of bereavement.

The loss of one's faith can also lead to a deep and unsettling loneliness, or the loss of a particular role or office within the community of faith. A retired minister may miss the vocation, social role and routine of ministry; a previously very active elder or volunteer may feel a loss of social interaction when that activity is no longer sustainable. William Cowper, the hymn writer, wrote of such losses in his hymn 'O for a Closer Walk with God', in which he likens spiritual loss to 'an aching void the world can never fill'.[3] ■

THINK

It might be worth considering that in the story of his prayers in Gethsemane, Jesus knew very clearly what he needed. Often when we are in a difficult situation we know what we need, but find that very hard to articulate or put into words. Think about a time when you had a real need for company; was there someone there for you? How did that individual meet your need? How did they know you were in need of their presence? How can you be sensitive to the signals other people put out to you when they specifically need your company?

READ

Read the story of Jesus needing his friends beside him in Matthew 26.36–46, paying particular attention in the story to what Jesus was suffering and to the need he had for both company and privacy.

These papers give an insight into people who might feel lonely today, perhaps while facing other serious life challenges:

Alison McCann, Phil Mackie and Ann Conacher, 'Isolation and Loneliness: What is the Scope for Public Health Action?', *Scottish Public Health Network Report*, May 2017, www.scotphn.net/wp-content/uploads/2017/05/2017_05_16-Loneliness-Scoping-Note-Final-formatted.pdf (accessed January 2018).

Marie Curie, 'Inequalities in Palliative Care – Isolation and Loneliness', *Marie Curie Briefing*, www.mariecurie.org.uk/globalassets/media/documents/policy/briefings-consultations/scotland-briefings/marie-curie-briefing-inequities-isolation-loneliness.pdf (accessed January 2018).

ACT

If you can hear a call in your community to meet the needs of the lonely, what could you do to answer that need? How could you enable people who might find it hard to put into words to tell you exactly what they want by way of services or volunteer support? Is there an organisation in your area already working with the lonely? If so, maybe you could join them or find a complementary service to offer in your pastoral care team.

3   William Cowper, 'O for a Closer Walk with God', in *Church Hymnary*, 4th edn (Norwich: Canterbury Press, 2005), 552.

LONELINESS AND ISOLATION:

The Poor in Spirit

Janet P. Foggie

Pioneer Minister, Church of Scotland Chaplain to the University of Stirling

Unlike loneliness, which refers to a feeling, isolation or social isolation is an objective state. Researchers can gather evidence of the number of people living in one-person households. They can calculate the distance to a town or post office, which is often the definition of rural isolation. Research questions concerning isolation tend to revolve around how often a person socialises, goes out in company or has visitors to the house.

In the Beatitudes Jesus says, 'Blessed are the poor in spirit, for theirs is the kingdom of heaven' (Matthew 5.3). The idea that if we are suffering from a poverty of spirit, or in some translations from poverty itself, God will care for us and the Christian community should look out for us is rooted in the Gospel. When we look at the effects of poverty on loneliness, the idea of chronic loneliness, and the 'window of loneliness', which is the perception of feeling alone, we see people in need who are a high priority for Christ.

Loneliness and poverty

Poverty is one of the highest priorities for the earthly ministry of Jesus Christ. He spoke often and frequently to the poor. He gave up his home and job to wander as a preacher. In the parable of the widow's mite, he uses the story of the wealthy man who can spare much as compared to the poor woman who 'gave all she had to live on'. Modern poverty, arguably, leads to more social isolation than in Jesus' day. The modern city is 'zoned' by the income of the inhabitants so much so that poverty is often described by postal codes. Bus links to the poorest areas are often inadequate and poverty leads to an inability to join in social activities that have a cost. Access to libraries, sports centres and community centres may be made more difficult by poverty.

Chronic loneliness

For those who are unable to work due to disability, are retired and are both socially isolated and feeling alone for more than a year or more, the term 'chronic loneliness' is applicable. The combination of ill health or physical disabilities with poverty can make it very difficult to be socially active. Feelings of loneliness can be made worse by a perception of stigma or a lack of transport to activities. It may take patience and time to enable these individuals to develop social interactions again.

The window of loneliness

For some, viewing the world through a 'window of loneliness' may be a very debilitating and difficult experience. Generalised anxiety disorder, social anxieties, depression or a diagnosis of a personality disorder or mental illness may create this 'frame' of feeling lonely, through which an individual sees all social interactions. Worry that an individual is not liked or not going to be liked in social situations may make it difficult to engage in those situations. This difficulty may then lead to a heightened feeling of loneliness. It is important for a pastoral carer to remember that loneliness is always a feeling and not to judge the loneliness of mental illness or poor mental wellbeing differently from other forms of loneliness. It is also key to recovery for the person with a diagnosis of a mental illness that they need to recognise, own and work on their unique symptoms with their care team if they have one. Judgements, advice or comments that are not sought by the individual who feels lonely in this way, are likely to make the situation worse, not better.

The mental health organisation Mind provides a very clearly written self-help guide, which gives some advice to enable individuals to decide what the cause of their loneliness might be. It is important that pastoral carers do not try to make these judgements for someone else, but instead guide people to the right resources in order to make decisions for themselves. This is the principle of empowerment and a significant source of good spiritual and mental wellbeing.

Rural isolation

Bearing in mind that isolation does not necessarily lead to feelings of loneliness, it is still reasonable to see a link between rural isolation and feelings of loneliness. Poor internet connections, long driving distances to basic facilities and fewer visitors to the house can contribute to rural isolation. For the older person in a rural area, there may be good community connections available through church, community or neighbours. But, a loss of the ability to drive or a loss of a key neighbour or friend may make a bigger difference to the isolated person's quality of life than might be the case in an urban setting.

The combination of ill health or physical disabilities along with poverty can make it very difficult to be socially active.

Pastoral care for chronic loneliness and isolation

The simple cure for loneliness might be getting people together, but it is important that this is thought through. For access to church, for example, an ability to hear might be essential to a good experience of worship; an ability to understand the spoken or written content might be a barrier; the physical ability to sit for an hour or to stand for a while might be challenging for a variety of reasons. Solving each of these in turn might be essential to everyone feeling included. Remember that some people can suffer an 'invisible' isolation or a feeling of isolation that is not perceived by the other people in the situation. An 'open door' on a Sunday morning is not sufficient to say that a church is 'inclusive'. Think about all the possible forms of loneliness and isolation as you walk around church on a Sunday morning and get groups of people together to decide what could be done to mitigate them.

There are many different ways of feeling lonely or being isolated. For each, though, the basic principles of pastoral care for the lonely and isolated are the same:

- Be aware of the consequences of prolonged feelings of loneliness on health.
- Be careful not to judge whether an individual is lonely or isolated for them, but instead to listen to them.
- Make sure community and church events are truly accessible, checking especially for 'invisible' barriers to the activity, such as deafness, poverty or social anxiety.
- Accept that some sources of loneliness, such as bereavement, cannot be 'fixed' but rather need time to mend even if they never heal completely.
- Always support people with poor mental wellbeing rather than advise or guide, empowering individuals to express for themselves how they are feeling and to choose for themselves what to do about it.

In prayer, in solitude, we remember that Jesus advised us to be alone sometimes. Loneliness is a human emotion that will always be part of our range of emotions. As Christians, we can offer love and companionship; we can work as members of society to end chronic loneliness. Yet, it would also be wise to acknowledge that some feelings of loneliness are part of who we are as God's creations. ∎

THINK

What did Jesus mean when he said, 'Blessed are the poor in spirit, for theirs is the kingdom of heaven' (Matthew 5.3)? Who is poor in spirit today? Who is poor in material terms? What other kinds of poverty of relationship might lead to feelings of loneliness? In what different ways might those individuals feel lonely? How could they benefit from more company?

READ

Read the Beatitudes in Matthew 5.1–12, looking at a variety of translations if you can, and notice the different words for poverty, poor in spirit or poor.

The following articles give an idea of what it is like for people coping with loneliness today:

Hardeep Aiden, *Trapped in a Bubble: An Investigation into the Triggers for Loneliness in the UK* (London: British Red Cross, 2017), www.redcross.org.uk/about-us/what-we-do/research-publications (accessed January 2018).

Mind, 'How to Cope with Loneliness', www.mind.org.uk/information-support/tips-for-everyday-living/loneliness/#.Wl4NF6hl-Uk (accessed January 2018).

ACT

One of the most important aspects of caring for people who might be suffering from loneliness and isolation is not to judge. Having an open mind and meeting people 'on the level' is sometimes a challenge.

Why not see if you can do some active listening and hear the stories of some people in your community who may be isolated or might feel lonely?

Alternatively, listen out for the lonely in unexpected places, instead of thinking that you know who is or isn't lonely. Why not ask the question of others, 'Are you feeling lonely?' and see what response you find.

MENTAL HEALTH STRUGGLES:

Stigma – Look Closer, See Me!

Cameron H. Langlands

Head of Spiritual and Pastoral Care, South London and Maudsley NHS Foundation Trust

'A diagnosis is burden enough without being burdened by secrecy and shame.' Jane Pauley[1]

Jane Pauley in the quotation above brings sharply into focus the nub of the issue around those who live daily with mental ill health. It is not the ill health, per se, that is the greatest burden they carry but instead the reaction to it of those around them. This reaction is similar in many ways to the one years ago when a cancer diagnosis was revealed.

The 'C' word would be whispered cautiously among family and friends for fear that the very uttering of it out loud would somehow unleash its power and thereby visit illness and devastation on families.

In many ways, then, mental ill health is the new cancer, and with it feelings of isolation and loneliness come all bound up in one word: *stigma*. From my time in parish ministry through to working in mental health chaplaincy, that one word hovers over many conversations that take place on a daily basis like a huge threatening, menacing black cloud enveloping all whose lives fall within its shadow.

If someone has an illness associated with any part of their body other than the brain they automatically receive sympathy. When it is the brain that is sick, however, often we do not know what to say, feeling uncomfortable and ill at ease. Due to this, the majority of people who suffer from mental ill health do not speak about their diagnosis because they are too ashamed. Instead, they put on a brave face; they hold their head up high and never tell a soul. It is the 'stiff upper lip' syndrome where we cannot be honest with others about our struggles because the shame and stigma keep us silent. In this silence, our humanity is denied and it leaves us feeling empty inside.

If we are being honest with ourselves, we have all faced being stigmatised at some point during our lives. It may be because we were not part of the 'in crowd', or we were not good at games and were always left until last when others were picked before us. It could be because of the way we look, the families we come from, our level of education or the way we speak. In the end, though, it all comes down to how we are perceived by others. When this was you, what happened? How did it make you feel? What impact did it have on you? In answering these

> ❝ It is not the ill health, per se, that is the greatest burden that they carry but instead the reaction to it of those around them.

1   'Out of the Shadows', *Journal Inquirer*, 2 May 2006, www.journalinquirer.com/archives/out-of-the-shadows-tv-personality-jane-pauley-tells-hartford/article_f2440820-9ef4-525a-ae73-a9503c6e62f3.html (accessed 13 May 2018).

questions, you may begin to gain a slight understanding of how those who struggle with their mental health feel and the devastating impact that the stigma associated with their illness has on their lives.

Those living with mental health issues often suffer from two forms of stigma. First, there is the external, where there is a difference in the way they are treated by others. This manifests itself, among other ways, in being avoided or given a wide berth, being judged for the way they behave, being discriminated against, being abused (verbally, physically or sexually) or being victimised. There is also a fear of stigma by association.

Second, there is the internal, which is inextricably bound up in the way the person is left feeling. Due to a combination of how they are feeling and how others treat them, people then often exclude themselves from a variety of social situations, struggle with perceptions of themselves, feel isolated and fear that others will find out about their diagnosis.

The impact of this is that the resultant avoidant behaviour, which isolates and divides, can cause people to withdraw from their social network of support, thereby putting them beyond the reach of badly needed support structures and services and helping to create a strong 'us' and 'them' culture.

We have got to retire these tired old narratives of the 'stiff upper lip', of 'being strong', of 'pulling ourselves together' and of 'not wanting to be a burden on others', because they are literally killing people. We have to learn that having feelings is not a sign of weakness, as feelings are what make us human. For when we deny our humanity, when we deny or have to hide who we truly are, it leaves an empty feeling inside.

Listening to the person who is ill helps, even if there is nothing else you feel able to do, as it enables them to gain the courage to share their story and regain some power over their personal narrative. By talking, those who are suffering in silence, in secrecy and in pain begin to realise that they are not alone and to know that with help and support they too can begin to heal.

Life is messy, unpredictable and tough and can lead us into places we would not ordinarily want to venture. But, with support we can help each other through it. I hope, in closing, that if your burden feels too heavy you will ask for help, and if you see someone struggling you will offer that listening ear. ∎

THINK
Think about how the congregation you are part of can engage better with those diagnosed with mental ill health.

READ
Read the stories of individuals whose lives have been affected by mental ill health and how they have sought to live with its consequences on the following websites: See Me (www.seemescotland.org); Time to Change (www.time-to-change.org.uk).

ACT
Why not hold a study evening on the topic of mental ill health? Invite a local mental health chaplain to speak about what they do and the challenges that are faced.

MENTAL HEALTH STRUGGLES:

Mental Ill Health - Listening

Cameron H. Langlands

Head of Spiritual and Pastoral Care, South London and Maudsley NHS Foundation Trust

'Perhaps the butterfly is proof that you can go through a great deal of darkness and still become something beautiful.' Unknown

At Easter, we had family come to stay for a few days. One morning my niece, who is about seven years old, was getting herself ready before we all headed out for a day exploring. She was brushing her teeth and as she did so the battery-operated toothbrush she was using slipped from her grip and hit one of her toes. A blood-curdling scream could be heard all over the house and we rushed to see what had happened. Through tears and caught breaths she relayed the story of what had occurred. Her toe was duly shown to all who were there and I could see nothing wrong with it. But, she still insisted on a plaster being put on it to make sure that her toe would be okay. In the moment that her toe was wrapped in a plaster, the crying subsided and her breathing became easier. She knew she was going to be okay.

This little girl, one who loves unicorns and muddy puddles, knows that she needs to brush her teeth to keep them healthy. She knows that a plaster makes you feel better when you have hurt your toe. She knows all about looking after her physical health. But, what does she know about looking after her psychological health? From childhood through adulthood, we are taught to take care of our physical health often to the detriment of our emotional health. Although our physical health appears to be so much more important – just look at the health magazines, the number of people on diets or the pressure the media put on young people to have the perfect body – statistics tell us that we are more likely to sustain psychological injuries than physical ones.

The most famous quotation about statistics is, 'There are three kinds of lies: lies, damned lies, and statistics.' It makes no difference, in reality, if it was American author Mark Twain or British Prime Minister Benjamin Disraeli who first coined the phrase. What matters is the sentiment that lies behind it. Statistics are everywhere you look and those regarding mental health are well known. We are reliably informed that one in four people will suffer from one form of mental health issue during their lives and that in the past week one in six people suffered from a common mental health problem. Statistics are helpful for highlighting the issues. But, in over twenty years of working in mental health chaplaincy, I have noticed that society appears to place more value in the body than it does the mind. Why is it that every other organ or body part can get sick and the person gets sympathy, except the brain?

Those who suffer from mental ill health do not have a condition as usually portrayed, namely the schizophrenic, the depressive, the eating disorder; they are people – your spouse, your partner, your child, your relative, your neighbour, your friend and your co-worker. They are people with hopes and dreams, just the same as you and me.

However, people with mental ill health often don't talk about their experience as they are fearful of the reaction they may encounter, such as conversations being stopped in their tracks. I once overheard someone say in reply to a person describing their illness, 'Oh, that's nice', simply because they did not know what to say. And this is the nub of the issue – what to say or not to say.

As we begin to engage with those who are suffering from mental ill health, the first rule of thumb is to make sure that you actually want to hear what they have to say. After all, surely there is nothing worse than telling someone how you truly feel with all the bravery that takes, only to be met by that person making it obvious through their body language and what they say that they would rather be anywhere else than sitting in front of you. For someone who often doesn't talk about their feelings or illness, a person who is not listening makes them feel as if they shouldn't be sharing their story. It makes them feel anxious, worried, useless, a burden.

But, in reality, when speaking with people suffering from mental ill health, what I hear them say is that they just want someone to listen to their story, to listen to where they are coming from and what they are experiencing; not to fix, give advice or tell them to pull themselves together, but rather to sit with them on the ash heap of their illness, listening, accompanying, being.

Being listened to is part of a person's healing and it can be incredibly cathartic to help someone to articulate something about their hopes, their dreams and their fears.

Being listened to is part of a person's healing and it can be incredibly cathartic to help someone to articulate something about their hopes, their dreams and their fears. It is more than making conversation, as truly listening shows genuine interest, shows that you see beyond the diagnosis, care about the person sitting in front of you and want to hear what they have to say. Listening is so much more than waiting to speak. It can be a scary place to be, but to truly listen can be a beautiful and incredibly therapeutic experience. ∎

THINK

What would make your congregation a welcoming one for those suffering from mental ill health and their relatives?

READ

Watch the following stories of those who have been affected by mental ill health and how they felt treated:

Mind, *Mental Health: In Our Own Words*, YouTube video, www.youtube.com/watch?v=_y97VF5UJcc.

Real Stories, *Breaking the Silence (Mental Health Documentary)*, YouTube video, www.youtube.com/watch?v=IMldOG37ARU.

ACT

Why not think about some members of your church undertaking mental first-aid training or a mindfulness course, and offering what they have learned to the congregation and community?

MY STORY

The Gerrie Family
Aberdeen

As a family, it was never easy to accept that our mum needed to go into a care home. However, as the symptoms of her dementia increased, we were slowly losing the ability to manage. With feelings of guilt and grieving for our mum, we had to make a decision.

Gratefully, Mum smiled as we stopped at the front door of Balmedie House. Entering the house for the first time, we could smell the lunch that reminded us of home, and the staff made us feel welcome.

That was nine years ago. During this time, Mum has built up a good friendship with the staff, as we also have. Often when we visited our mum the staff enabled us to get involved in the care of her in various ways. This would help Mum to be assured of our love and care for her. It also helped us feel that we were still an active part of her care.

As Mum's journey of dementia has gradually affected her physical and mental ability, there have been times we have been worried that her needs would no longer be able to be met. However, the staff at Balmedie had a good understanding of what was important to Mum. Their compassionate approach, which demonstrated that they recognise our mum as a person and not the symptoms of the illness, relieved our anxiety and provided reassurance that she would have a quality of life we never thought would be possible. She would fulfil everything on her bucket list by attending a baking session, taking part in games, and so on.

Over the recent years, Mum's health has been more of a concern. When we have visited her, we have thought that it could be our last day with her. However, each time Mum has recovered, thanks to the loving care of the staff. We are sure that our mum is like a cat; she certainly has nine lives. She will continue to enjoy company and feel loved, surrounded by people who care. ■

DEMENTIA:

Understanding Dementia

John Swinton
Chair in Divinity and Religious Studies, University of Aberdeen

The pastoral care of people living with dementia is in many ways no different from the ways in which we might care for anyone within our church communities. All of us need such things as love, responsive presence, affirmation and positive recognition if we are to flourish. All of us need to be helped to find ways to remain in relationship with God, self and others in all circumstances and at all times. That is as so for people with dementia as it is for all members of Jesus' body. Dementia does, however, draw out some quite specific challenges for Church and society, but perhaps not in the ways we might assume. A significant proportion of the disablement that people living with dementia experience is caused by people's attitudes towards them and a variety of misunderstandings about what dementia actually is and what it means to live well with dementia. Dementia is certainly a neurological condition, but it is much more than that. In a culture that places a high value on such things as memory, intellect, reason, clear-mindedness, fitness, competitiveness and speed of thought, being in a position where one appears to be losing such abilities can become highly problematic. So much so that some mistakenly assume that damage to one's brain is damage to one's personhood. When we say things like, 'She is not the person she used to be', we implicitly or explicitly suggest that the person living with dementia is not really a person at all. But, if she is not the person she used to be, then who is she? If she is not a person at all, as some would argue, then why would we love her? If we don't think she is the person she used to be, then why would we care for this 'stranger'?

Thinking differently

We can, however, think differently about dementia. If someone were to encounter dementia within a community and a culture that valued and prioritised such things as love, care, friendship, fidelity, relationships, community and belonging, many of the issues of stigmatisation and alienation faced by people living with dementia would look quite different. They wouldn't go away, of course. But we would see and respond to them differently. The Church should be precisely such a community.

As Christians, we know that people are not simply their brains. In the Genesis account of creation, God blows God's breath into dust and creates a whole human being (Genesis 2.7). God does not simply create a brain! We are whole people created by a Holy God who sees us in the splendour of our wholeness no matter what our circumstances may be. Human beings are relational creatures; we find our identity – who we are – not just by thinking about who we are or by remembering who we are. We discover who we are in and through the various relationships that we encounter in life. That relational process goes on even in the midst of significant brain damage. We always and necessarily need one another to remind us of who we are. The apostle Paul tells us that who we are is not about our memory but about God's memory. Jesus will never forget us or abandon us:

> For I am convinced that neither death, nor life, nor angels, nor rulers, nor things present, nor things to come, nor powers, nor height, nor depth, nor anything else in all creation, will be able to separate us from the love of God in Christ Jesus our Lord. (Romans 8.38–39)

There is nothing in Scripture to indicate that this passage does not also apply to people living with dementia.

Dementia is, of course, a complicated neurological condition.[1] It is, however, first and foremost a profound human experience that occurs within the lives of unique individuals who are valued and valuable and who desire to have lives that are full and fruitful. In John 10.10, Jesus tells us that he has come to bring life in all its fullness. This does not change when someone encounters brain damage. People sometimes talk negatively about people living with dementia: 'I would hate to be like that.' 'Life wouldn't be worth living without memory.' Apart from the obvious questions – 'How would you know?' – such language indicates the way people can easily forget that the person living with dementia remains a person no matter what, who still desires to live life to the full even amid the changes. The language we use mirrors what we think we are looking at. If we see someone as a person and talk about them as a person, we will treat them as a person. If we see someone as a non-person, we will speak and act accordingly. Pastoral care requires a renewing of our minds (Romans 12.2) in order that our vision can shift from problems to persons and from hopelessness towards new relational possibilities now and into the future. The simple gift of recognising the worth of a person and offering friendship and support is the beginning point for faithful pastoral care.

---

1   Readers interested in finding out more on this should visit the website of Alzheimer's Scotland: www.alzscot.org/information_and_resources/information_sheet/1748_what_is_dementia.

> " The simple gift of recognising the worth of a person and offering friendship and support is the beginning point for faithful pastoral care.

Discipleship and dementia

It is important to recognise that these unique and deeply valuable people who live with dementia do not cease to be disciples simply because they have brain damage. Some worry that because people are forgetting things about themselves, others and God, they will somehow cease to be followers of Jesus. But that fear is not justified. God does not abandon us because we forget things. It's not what we know that makes us disciples. It is not our knowledge or our memories that matter, but the continuing call of Jesus. Dietrich Bonhoeffer noted that when Matthew was called by Jesus, he didn't actually know who Jesus was. We could imagine that Matthew had heard stories about Jesus or seen the things he had done. However, there is nothing in the biblical text to suggest that that is the case. Jesus called and Matthew followed. Indeed, for most of the time Jesus' disciples didn't know who Jesus was! But they remained disciples. If it is the case that nothing can separate us from the love of God and if it is true that the Spirit speaks in groans that cannot be understood (Romans 8.26), then we can be assured that God does not forget or abandon us even when we can't remember, understand or articulate things in the way we used to. A key pastoral task is to help the Church to remember that when we talk about pastoral care with people living with dementia, we are talking about the ways in which we can enable disciples living with dementia to feel the love of God and hold onto the essence of the call of Jesus to 'Follow me'.

Dementia as a neurological condition

The neurological aspect of a person's experience comprises such things as changes to memory, together with alterations in behaviour, cognition and social functioning. There are different types of dementia which manifest themselves in different ways. The changes people experience differ depending on which part of the brain has been damaged, and the symptoms and behaviours change as the disease progresses. Different skills and abilities and lifelong habits may remain while others are distorted and changed by the condition. People do change and we need to think about ways in which all of us together can constructively adapt to these changes. However, it is important to place these changes in the correct context. Dementia is first and foremost a change in a person's story. It is a story of sadness, loss and lament. But, it is also a story that contains new possibilities and opportunities for creative innovation, if we can find the right kind of imagination to enable such things. Creating new, hopeful stories for and with people is the essence of the Gospel and the heart of dementia care. ■

THINK

Reflect on the kind of language you use when you are speaking about people living with dementia.

Think about the way in which people talk about dementia within your congregation. Is it positive or is it negative? Why?

Think about what it might mean to suggest that someone with advanced dementia is a disciple and still has a calling from God to participate in what God is doing within the Church.

READ

Alzheimer's Society, 'About Dementia', www.scie.org.uk/dementia/about/.

Alzheimer's Society, 'What not to say to someone with dementia', blog.alzheimers.org.uk/dementia-insight/language-dementia-what-not-to-say/.

Albert Jewell, ed., *Spirituality and Personhood in Dementia* (London: Jessica Kingsley, 2011).

John Swinton, *Dementia: Living in the Memories of God* (Grand Rapids, MI: Eerdmans, 2012).

ACT

Spend some time with a person living with dementia and try to understand what it is that makes their lives feel worthwhile.

Spend some time with someone who has a family member living with dementia and try to understand what might be useful in terms of help and support.

Invite a person with dementia to come to church with you.

DEMENTIA:

Possibilities for Pastoral Care

John Swinton
Chair in Divinity and Religious Studies, University of Aberdeen

With the thoughts in the previous article in mind, we can now begin to think about what kind of approaches we might develop in order to help create new stories and to minister faithfully to those living with dementia.

People living with dementia

Throughout the previous article, I have used the term 'people living with dementia'. This is partly to enable readers always to remember that it is people that we are talking about and partly to emphasise the idea of living with and living well. But the term is not confined to the individual who lives with brain damage. The term relates to a wide range of people who are connected to that individual: family, friends, neighbours, communities, towns and cities. In this sense, *all of us* are people living with dementia. Understood in this way, the focus of pastoral care can never be restricted to a matter of one-to-one encounters (important as such encounters are). It always and inevitably needs to take into consideration the community within which a person lives and how that community can be mobilised to care. *Pastoral care with people living with dementia is not just in one aspect of its ministry. It is something the Church does together.*

Speaking properly

A first step towards faithful pastoral care is for the Church always to be mindful of its language. As a community, we must learn to speak thoughtfully and compassionately about dementia and those living with it. The words that we use to describe something create the worlds that we think we see. The world we think we see determines how we respond to the things we see in the world. A simple but key task of pastoral care is to help the Church as a community to speak appropriately about dementia and to help people living with dementia to remain remembered for who they *are in the present* as they look towards a meaningful future.

Visiting

One of the major problems that people living with dementia experience is *loneliness*. Because of the stigma and negative thinking that goes on around dementia, people's friendships very often fade away. It is not uncommon to hear people say such things as, 'I never visit him. I prefer to remember him the way he was.' Such a response leaves the person with dementia alone and abandoned by her community. The solution to such loneliness is fairly straightforward: *visit people*. In Matthew 25, Jesus informs us that those who visit the sick, the alienated, the outcast are actually visiting him. The simple act of visiting someone turns out to be a deep act of worship. Offering the gift of your time is a profound gift. *The gift of time is healing.*

Worship and learning to be in the moment

Worshipping with people living with advanced dementia is profoundly important. It is as we worship that we encounter people in new ways. Through the songs, the prayers or the music, people living with dementia will often participate in ways that they don't do at other moments of their lives. It would be easy to read such participation sentimentally as vestiges of a past spiritual life. But to do that would be a mistake. Sometimes with dementia it is not that a memory has been lost. Rather, the neural pathways to the brain are damaged in such a way as to block access to the memory. When one neural pathway is blocked, the brain uses other neural pathways to compensate. So when you see someone sing and respond in worship, it may be that they are accessing a memory that is simply not available without the presence of music and the usage of those neural pathways. When we sing, we experience all sorts of things. Music contains memories, hopes, experiences and relationships. But when the music stops, so does the memory. The key pastoral task within the context of worship is to learn how to be with someone in that moment; how to engage with the person as they remember, always bearing in mind that we may be there only for this moment, but this moment is deeply precious. There is a frustration and a disappointment in this. Like Peter on the mountain top with Jesus, Elijah and Moses, we want this moment to last for ever. Effective worship, like effective visiting, means learning to be present in the moment.

new opportunities emerge for growth and living well even in the midst of the most difficult of challenges.

Lament and joy

I have tried to indicate some positive ways of looking at and truly being with people living with dementia. I would not, however, wish to avoid the fact that there is also deep suffering, loss, grief and disappointment that accompanies dementia. It is not an easy road for any of us. If we are to care faithfully, we need to learn how to. Lament is a form of prayer that expresses sadness, grief, disappointment, anger and hope. There are more psalms of lament in the Bible than any other kind. God clearly wants us to be honest in prayer. The structure of the Psalms is key. Psalm 13 runs like this:

> How long, Lord? Will you forget me for ever?
> How long will you hide your face from me?
> How long must I wrestle with my thoughts
> and day after day have sorrow in my heart?
> How long will my enemy triumph over me?
> Look on me and answer, Lord my God.
> Give light to my eyes, or I will sleep in death,
> and my enemy will say, 'I have overcome him,'
> and my foes will rejoice when I fall.
> But I trust in your unfailing love;
> my heart rejoices in your salvation.
> I will sing the Lord's praise,
> for he has been good to me. (NIV)

The lament begins with an outpouring of grief, loss, frustration and anger. But then, in the middle of the psalm, something changes. For whatever reason, the psalmist changes his perspective as he remembers God's unfailing love. Nothing has changed in terms of his suffering, but now he sees things differently – more hopefully. This allows him to worship even in the midst of his sorrow. Lament is a prayerful way for us to express and articulate our sadness and disappointment within a context that is deeply hopeful. Enabling people living with dementia, carers and support workers to be honest about their sadness, while at the same time recognising the presence of hope, is a vital task of pastoral care for those living with dementia.

Pastoral care that is located within the hopefulness of the Gospel opens up fresh possibilities for seeing people differently and responding in ways that are sensitive, life-enhancing and spiritual in their very core. In this article, I have tried to indicate some of the ways of *looking at* and *truly seeing* people living with dementia that underpin the practices of faithful pastoral care. When we learn to look with our hearts and care with a passion for people living with dementia, new opportunities emerge for growth and living well even in the midst of the most difficult of challenges. ■

THINK

How would I like to be treated if I have dementia?

What kinds of things can we do to enable people with dementia to remain loved and remembered?

How can the worship within my congregation be made more accessible for people living with dementia?

READ

Louise Morse, *Worshipping with Dementia: Meditations, Scriptures and Prayers for Sufferers and Carers* (London: Monarch, 2010).

Trevor Adams, *Developing Dementia-friendly Churches* (Cambridge: Grove Booklets, 2017).

Joanna Collicutt, *Thinking of You: A Resource for the Spiritual Care of People with Dementia* (London: Bible Reading Fellowship, 2017).

ACT

Offer to visit and spend time with a family living with dementia.

Think about ways in which your congregation can be encouraged to visit people in care homes.

Create a liturgy that includes the experiences of people living with dementia.

CARING FOR THE TERMINALLY ILL AND THEIR LOVED ONES:

Awareness of Self

Ewan Kelly
Associate Minister of Queen's Park Govanhill Parish Church, Glasgow

Pastoral care as being

Offering pastoral care to someone who is terminally ill or dying, or to their loved ones, is essentially the same as caring for anyone else. We utilise the same gifts and abilities and the same approach to caring. Yet, paradoxically, it is profoundly not the same. Why? Because in doing so we are confronted by our own mortality and the mortality of those we love. Frances Dominica was the driving force behind the first children's hospice in the UK. For her, pastoral care of the dying and their families is about listening more than speaking, being present for as long as is welcomed and having the courage to be ourselves and thus allow the other(s) to feel safe to be themselves too.[1] The courage to be who we are is dependent on our awareness of who we are and what we bring to each pastoral encounter.

Self-awareness and intentional use of self

Areas to be particularly aware of as we seek to care for those living with terminal illness or dying include the following.

Our mortal self

To what depth have any of us considered our own mortality? As we live, we are also ageing and dying. Psalm 90.12 reminds us to 'count our days that we may gain a wise heart'. A deepening realisation that there truly is an end to our earthly existence as well as beginning may in and of itself heighten meaning and purpose in our lives. However, to contemplate such is to reflect on leaving behind all that is good and worthwhile in our earthly existence, including the love of family and friends. On the face of it, it is no wonder that most of us are reticent to engage in such activity. However, our lives are full of little deaths or losses, for example endings of relationships, roles, projects at work or church, and leaving places or homes. Learning to embrace movement and change and the lessons learned from such experiences can enrich our lives and living. James Woodward talks of such 'befriending death' as an opportunity, 'which encourages us to self-correction, self-formation and self-expression'.[2] Moreover, engaging in such a process may free us up to risk journeying with others who are facing death and its associated transitions more imminently. To journey with those facing death in the near future is also to bump into the process of dying and the pain and suffering that we may fear for ourselves or our loved ones.

How would we like to die, or perhaps more to the point, how would we not? What about the mode of death for those close to us? Would we want them to die suddenly without saying goodbye or have time to say goodbye but risk a lingering death? What are our fears, previously expressed or hidden, based on our own experience of death and dying? Gently exploring these questions for ourselves may help us to be a less anxious presence when others need to explore their anxieties and fears in our company.

Suffering self

Offering pastoral care to those facing death and dying is to accompany, not to fix, advise or correct. We are not there 'to tell them how they should think or behave, but to stay with them while they discover the answers within themselves'.[3] In order to provide others with a non-judgemental space in which to wrestle with issues of physical, emotional and existential suffering and where God might be in their experience, we need to have some awareness and understanding of our own beliefs and perspectives. Are we comfortable enough with our own faith in, and doubts and questions about, God in relation to human suffering to enable us to hold a space for others where they can question or even rage with or about God in relation to their situation? Can we do so without having to defend God or trying to work through our own questions within that space? (The latter needs to be done at some other time and in another safe place with a trusted other, where the focus is our self and not those we care for.)

Self and life after death

Similarly, to what extent have we thought about what happens after death? Not just any death – our death. What is it that we believe and how aware are we of the range of beliefs that people may have? Physical or 'spiritual' resurrection? Or is death the end? What about immortality of the soul or reincarnation? Again, our role as pastoral carers is not to convince or argue but to enable people to explore their hopes, fears and questions and allow the provisional and the exploratory to be, without fear of judgement or critical comment. To be an accepting loving presence in the face of such does require us to have thought about our beliefs and be honest with ourselves about the questions and doubts we might have.

1 Frances Dominica, *Just My Reflection: Helping Parents to Do Things Their Way When Their Child Dies* (London: Darton, Longman & Todd, 1997).
2 James Woodward, *Befriending Death* (London: SPCK, 2005), 74.
3 Dominica, *Just My Reflection*, xx.

Limited self

In addition to the normal limitations we may feel and experience in pastoral relationships, when we are supporting the terminally ill, the dying and their loved ones, there may be an accentuated feeling of helplessness. Things may be happening to people we care about and they may be suffering in ways we find difficult to bear, and which are way beyond our control. This is hard. Are we able to notice our dis-ease with such feelings and allow them to be? Again, talking them over with a trusted other or in a pastoral care group is important to help us live with and understand the source of these feelings.

Transformed self

With reflection and support, journeying with those living with terminal illness and imminent death can help us learn more about ourselves and grow in our journey of faith.

An awareness of our life being a gift of a limited timescale rather than a right to ongoing health and longevity may enable us to embrace life more fully in the present and all that each moment may offer us. Such an approach may not only heighten our attentiveness in relationships with others and open us to all that we may receive as well as offer, it may also enhance our relationships with the wonder of the natural world, the arts and ourselves. In all of these, in such moments of mindfulness and times of full immersion in our human interactions and experience, we may glimpse something of God.[4] ■

> ## " An awareness of our life being a gift of a limited timescale . . . may enable us to embrace life more fully

THINK

Read Ecclesiastes 3.19–20 and reflect on this question: If we thought and spoke more about death and dying as part of normal life, how might it help us as individuals, families and communities to deal with death and dying when they happen?

Reflect on this sentence, which emerges from the context of healthcare: 'Death may be postponed, even avoided, but not ultimately evaded.'[5]

Read Stewart Conn's poem, 'Visiting Hour'.[6] When have you felt like that? How did you deal with those feelings?

READ

James Woodward, *Befriending Death* (London: SPCK, 2005).

Ewan Kelly, *Personhood and Presence: Self as a Resource for Spiritual and Pastoral Care* (London: T & T Clark, 2012), especially Chapter 8, 'Mortal Self'.

Sheila Cassidy, *Sharing the Darkness* (London: Darton, Longman & Todd, 2002).

ACT

Plan your own funeral, and discuss it with your loved ones if you have not done so.

Write your own obituary.

Discuss with others in your church and community the possibility of running an event to raise death awareness, such as a 'death cafe'.[7]

4   Ewan Kelly, *Personhood and Presence: Self as a Resource for Spiritual and Pastoral Care* (London: T & T Clark, 2012), 139.
5   Church of Scotland, *Euthanasia: A Christian Perspective* (Edinburgh: Saint Andrew Press, 1997).
6   Stewart Conn, 'Visiting Hour', https://clodandpebble.wordpress.com/2012/07/11/visiting-hour-by-stewart-conn/ (accessed 2 March 2018).
7   Good Life, Good Death, Good Grief, 'Death Awareness Week', www.goodlifedeathgrief.org.uk/blogs/awareness-week-2017/ (accessed 2 March 2018).

CARING FOR THE TERMINALLY ILL AND THEIR LOVED ONES:

Pastoral Responses or Actions

Ewan Kelly
Associate Minister of Queen's Park Govanhill Parish Church, Glasgow

Embodiment

As we visit the terminally ill or dying or their loved ones, we may represent or embody different things for different people. The world for those who are living with terminal illness or impending death is smaller than when they were well. They have less energy, are less able to concentrate, and their focus becomes naturally narrower: on self, family and close friends. Work colleagues, neighbours, fellow church members and acquaintances may become peripheral to their 'cone of awareness'.[1] Depending on the situation and our previous relationship with them, when we visit we may, therefore, represent the wider world. Our presence may be welcomed as a break from the intensity of the situation, or perhaps be an unwanted intrusion. Sensitivity to body language and what is not said, as well as what is, is important in informing how we respond. People may welcome us as a representative of God and/or the Church, or they may project their feelings of anger, questioning and despair that they may have about God in their current situation onto us. How we are with them and how we relate in response embodies something of God. People asking questions to God or about God are not looking for magic answers from us but for our non-judgemental company – as someone they trust who will stay with them for as long as is wanted as they wrestle and express their feelings. In doing so, we embody the loving, compassionate presence of Christ, as we help to normalise such activity and enable people to feel that they have permission to grieve their dying or their dying loved one healthily (see also the 'Listening' section below). Having the honesty and courage to say, 'I don't know' when we don't have the answer is helpful in facilitating this process.

Listening

Allowing people to talk about what they want or say what they need to is important. Often people may not want to talk about deep and meaningful or difficult stuff, especially straight away. They might want to talk about more ordinary or mundane things, or things they most value: their daily routine, the weather, the garden, football, *Strictly Come Dancing* or their family or ours. We may help to bring a touching point with the wider world and a sense of some sort of normality into their lives. People who are aware that their condition is terminal and are dying, or people who are caring for them, are in the process of anticipatory grieving. They are trying to get their heads round layers of loss and seeking to make sense of their lives, relationships and all they are currently dealing with as well as their impending death. Many will be wondering where God is in all of this. This can be potentially overwhelming for all concerned. Grieving is a social as well as a physical, emotional and spiritual process. For many people, the opportunity to talk about significant aspects of their life story can be potentially healing – helping them find some sort of meaning in their life or legacy that they feel they may be leaving behind. In addition, it may enable people to name and perhaps deal with any unfinished business, including relationship issues.

---

1   Ian Ainsworth-Smith and Peter Speck, *Letting Go: Caring for the Dying and Bereaved*, 2nd edn (London: SPCK, 1999), 37.

"

The world for those who are living with terminal illness or impending death is smaller than when they were well.

Speaking

Use of the Bible

For some Christians, hearing the Bible read to them, especially at times of uncertainty and transition, may be very important. Some people may ask us spontaneously to read particular passages from Scripture of comfort and hope for them. However, like prayer, Scripture should be used thoughtfully. It is important to ask others if this is something they might find helpful; avoid assumptions and respond to cues they give us in conversation. Whose need is being met by reading the Bible is a useful question to ask ourselves. It may be easier for us to do something in a situation where we feel helpless or to prevent our exposure to raw feelings and our own mortality rather than simply being with another and listening. Referring to biblical stories in our pastoral conversations can be especially helpful when people are struggling with their anger and questioning of God. To do so is not a bad Christian witness or to fail some way in our faith. It is biblical, Christ-like and normal. Making reference to Psalm 22, Job's questioning and Jesus' feelings of abandonment on the cross may be reassuring and permissive.

Prayer

As in other pastoral situations, sensitive prayers emerge out of a pastoral conversation and include (with honesty and courage) the feelings, longings, beliefs and the questions that are expressed verbally and non-verbally in the time together. It is generally good practice to keep prayers short and to the point.

Doing

Touch can convey God's love, solidarity and compassion, especially when words feel inadequate: the clasp of a hand or a hand on an arm or shoulder or a hug if appropriate. The ideal is that the other takes our hand.[2] Use touch only when we sense the other is comfortable with it and so are we. Be sensitive to issues of gender, age and power. Be aware that touch can be perceived as an intimate expression, especially if we are on our own with the other. Whose need will be met by touching?

Leaving

Visits to those who are terminally ill or dying are best kept short. Dying or living with terminal illness can be a very lonely time, so a return visit may well be greatly appreciated. Remember that when you leave, the Holy Spirit fills the space you have left; you never leave people alone.[3] What are you going to do for yourself once you have left? Such visits are draining. How are you going to redress your balance? ■

2   Bob Whorton, *Reflective Caring: Imaginative Listening to Pastoral Experience* (London: SPCK, 2011).

3   Read John 16.7. If we believe we embody the love and care of Christ in a pastoral situation, perhaps Jesus' words to his friends, 'If I do not go the advocate will not come', may help us to let go and hand over an individual or family into God's care. For when we leave, the Helper fills the space we have left.

THINK

Read Psalm 22.1–21 and Matthew 27.45–50, or Psalm 143. How might these readings inform any pastoral care of the dying or terminally ill you may provide?

How able are you to remain quiet and be still? How often are you still and quiet in your daily life? How easy is it to listen to another if we don't make space for silence to listen to ourselves and God?

Think of times when you have been struggling in life and someone has held your hand, put an arm round your shoulder or given you a hug? How did that feel? How might this reflection inform your pastoral care?

What might be the role of prayer in pastoral care of the terminally ill and the dying?

READ

Bob Whorton, *Reflective Caring: Imaginative Listening to Pastoral Experience* (London: SPCK, 2011).

Tom Gordon, *A Need for Living: Signposts on the Journey of Life and Beyond* (Glasgow: Wild Goose Publications, 2001).

Good Life, Good Death, Good Grief (www.goodlifedeathgrief. org.uk/content/online_resources).

ACT

Gather together your local pastoral care group or interested parties from your church and watch one or two of the films sharing the stories of those living with life-limiting conditions on the Good Life, Good Death, Good Grief website (www. goodlifedeathgrief.org.uk/content/films). Have a discussion about your response to the films.

If you are providing support to the dying, terminally ill and/or their loved ones, meet regularly with trusted and experienced others to reflect on your pastoral practice.

Invite a chaplain from a local health board or hospice to come and hold a learning session in your church about pastoral care of those living with dying and life-limiting conditions.

BEREAVEMENT:

Common Misconceptions

Tom Gordon

Former Chaplain, Marie Curie Hospice Edinburgh

Hurting, confused and broken people often find it hard to access appropriate support in their bereavement and find that they are increasingly confused, uncertain and isolated in their grief. Dealing appropriately with grief, loss and bereavement is, therefore, crucial to pastoral work in congregation and parish. This article and the following offer insight into the needs of bereaved people and some suggestions on offering workable and accessible care and support. We have to begin, however, by clarifying some common misconceptions.

It is a misconception to believe that reaction to loss is always linear

When the Swiss/American psychiatrist Elisabeth Kübler-Ross looked at bereavement issues, she informed us that:

- Reactions to bereavement need to be accepted as normal.
- There are patterns of human behaviour that are predictable.
- We can see in one person's response to loss what we've already seen in others.
- Models of grief can be understood, spoken about and offered as reassurance to bereaved people.

In 1969, she published *On Death and Dying*[1] and postulated for the first time the Kübler-Ross model, the 'five stages of grief', a series of emotions experienced by terminally ill patients or those who are bereaved: denial, anger, bargaining, depression and acceptance. This model was quickly accepted by the general public and medical professionals. But it also caused problems: first, it was too easy for bereaved people to be labelled at arbitrary stages of grief; second, such a linear theory was then taught to generations of medical students.

" the stages of grief are a collation of common experiences that can occur in any order, if at all.

Loss *would* be understood to follow a 'healing' pattern, like bowel surgery, a leg-break or radiotherapy. But, research shows that the stages of grief are *not* a linear and predictable progression. Rather, they are a collation of common experiences that can occur in any order, if at all.

In recent years, grief theories have helpfully become more flexible and include the following:[2]

- John Bowlby's 'attachment theory' (1969, 1973), based, for the first time, on empirical evidence
- Colin Murray Parkes' 'shifting pictures'
- William Worden's 1992 theory, 'the tasks of mourning'
- Klass, Silverman and Nickman's 'continuing bonds' from 1996
- Stroebe and Schut's 'dual process model' at the turn of the century.

It is a misconception to expect most reactions to grief to be abnormal

It is important that manifestations of grief are normalised. In all losses, we search for a 'new normal'. But when we don't know what that is, we question whether our reactions to loss, which look abnormal, are appropriate or not. So, normality has to be checked out and responded to with reassurance both from professionals and from the experiences of others who are bereaved and react in the same way.

We must adjust our parameters and widen our preprogrammed spectrum of normality. When we're trained to recognise abnormalities, we'll look for them first and so *narrow* our understanding of the ways people react to loss. But when we widen our parameters and include more people in our spectrum of normality, better support is possible.[3]

It is a misconception to assume that society's attitudes to death are getting better

Society's attitudes to death and our tolerance and understanding of bereavement are getting worse. Two decades ago, the remarkable public reaction to the death of Princess Diana seemed to illustrate a change in our reaction to death. And many have said that we're more open about our grief and more understanding and accepting than we used to be; the

1　Elisabeth Kübler-Ross, *On Death and Dying* (Abingdon: Routledge, 1969).

2　For more on current grief theories, see Tom Gordon, Ewan Kelly and David Mitchell, eds, *Spiritual Care for Healthcare Professionals* (London: Radcliffe, 2011), 112–24.

3　For an exploration of aspects of grief and stories about how real people have dealt with these, see Tom Gordon, *New Journeys Now Begin: Learning on the Path of Grief and Loss* (Glasgow: Wild Goose Publications, 2007).

stiff upper lip has gone. While that may be true in the public arena, it is not translated into an understanding and acceptance of private grief in personal loss.

There is, for example, the ever shorter time frame in which exhibiting reactions to loss are considered acceptable. Bereaved people are expected to 'act the part' of having recovered from grieving sooner than they are ready for. As a result, they find themselves pushed further into isolation, confusion and self-doubt.

Then, there's the 'pecking order of grief', where some losses are deemed to be more challenging and more likely to create obvious signs of grieving than others. From a suicide – unspeakably awful – *down* the pecking order to the unremarkable death of a friend or neighbour – 'Why are you not coming back to work after the funeral?'

Bereaved people are also victims of the noticeable dismantling of community and the parallel increase in individualism. From churches to the Miners' Welfare Club, they don't feel they 'belong' any more. So, in loss there are diminishing opportunities for a community to show or offer expressions of understanding and care.

Allied to this, there's the loss of 'modelling' in our society. How do people know whether their reactions are okay? Curtains aren't closed following a death. There's seldom a cortege to the funeral. Men don't doff their hats as a hearse passes. There are no 'widow's weeds' and fewer black ties. Where do we find models of appropriate responses to bereavement, or even a concern that we are bereaved at all?

And finally, there's the 'let's get on' attitude, with bereaved people all too quickly having to live in two worlds, one of grief and one of coping, and experience the painfulness, for a long time, of the transition from one to the other.

Is society better able to deal with bereavement now? I'm not at all sure.

Let's be careful to face up to misconceptions, and thus approach loss, grief and bereavement in a more informed way. Let's be caring and thorough in our attempts to understand and respond to the needs of those who are bereaved. ∎

THINK

Think about your own circumstances and understanding of bereavement. Are there issues in your own journeys of loss that need to be explored before you seek to offer support to others?

How easy is it for us to be patient and helpful companions to bereaved people for a longer period than they or we expect? How comfortable are we in offering a different understanding – and timescale – to society's way of coping with death?

READ

As well as the publications referenced in the footnotes, it is worth looking at:

Henri Nouwen, *The Wounded Healer* (London: Darton, Longman & Todd, 2014), for self-help and insight as a carer.

Jane Morrell and Simon Smith, *We Need to Talk About the Funeral: 101 Practical Ways to Commemorate and Celebrate Life* (Cardiff: Accent Press, 2007), on issues relating to funerals.

Lezley Stewart, *Celebrating Life in Death* (Edinburgh: Saint Andrew Press, 2016), on funerals, thanksgiving and remembering.

ACT

Consider the provision in your locality of bereavement support. If there is little or nothing, ask what might be done to offer more support for those who are bereaved.

Think about what your church is already doing through the minister, deacon, elders and the like, and what could be done to enhance and develop this.

Consider carefully what kind of bereavement support might be appropriate for your locality.

BEREAVEMENT:

Things that can Make a Difference

Tom Gordon

Former Chaplain, Marie Curie Hospice Edinburgh

Before we explore what can make a difference in bereavement, it would be helpful to highlight a number of problem approaches:[1]

- The 'fixing' approach: when we think that everything can be made better. It's wrong to expect that no matter what intervention is offered it will lead to betterment and that sadness can be stopped. We like it when people say they're 'over it' or have 'moved on' so that we can be satisfied with what we've helped achieve. But we can't *fix* loss.
- The 'too-limited' approach: when we only have one model of bereavement support in our experience, usually a one-to-one approach. In our churches, it's the 'visiting model', individual and home-based. In society, it's the assurance that 'counsellors are available'. And in both Church and society, there's the danger of abrogating our responsibility by placing the support process in the hands of those trained to deal with it.
- The 'judgemental' approach: when we criticise people who are not coping as well as we expect them to. If bereaved people are not showing signs of progress (whatever these are), they are often labelled, or perceive themselves to be labelled, as problematic or less than adequate. How honest are we, for example, about how bereavement challenges our faith, when well-meaning people might make us feel that doubts, questions and struggles are signs of a failure to be good enough Christians?
- The 'lack-of-understanding' approach: when we think loss is *only* about coping with death. But the same reactions are prevalent – and often more so – in all losses: divorce, a house fire, redundancy, a scandal, the loss of a limb, dementia and much more (see the 'Who am I Now?' section below).

So, how might we make a difference?

We make a difference when we give bereaved people a chance to talk

People look for ways of masking the pain of their loss: being busy, saying they're fine, drinking too much, seeking medical interventions, and so on. If they're isolated in the processing of that pain and hide it even from those who love them the most, their struggle is exacerbated. People need a chance to talk and be listened to.

For too long in churches, bereavement support has been left to the minister or deacon – the professional church worker – and limited to a one-to-one approach. But not all ministers and deacons are adequately equipped to understand, far less offer, good bereavement care; training, personality, theology and lack of self-knowledge are all factors. Now we must look to the ministry of the *whole* people. Of course, there are a number of issues to get right, such as adequate training, confidentiality, quality control and trust. However, if these are clarified, there is a firm foundation for our work.

In recent years, churches have begun to use a group-based model. When bereaved people are brought together, rather than everyone disappearing into a black hole of sorrow or hopelessness, they feel *less* isolated. One person's story articulates another's needs. One person's yearnings find empathy in another's tears. One person's anger finds acceptance in another's thanks. One person's pain finds healing in another's love. It's a forum for sharing and being listened to, included, normalised and not judged.

This is the model offered in my own church. It's called 'Stepping Stones', which is based on the 'Acorns' programmes. We offer two six-week support programmes a year in the local community centre run by a team of eight trained, supported and valued members of the congregation.[2] A group-based model deals with isolation, and offers an accepting, encouraging and confidence-building experience. It works!

---

1   For an exploration of various aspects of end-of-life care, including bereavement and stories of people facing these issues, see Tom Gordon, *A Need for Living: Signposts on the Journey of Life and Beyond* (Glasgow: Wild Goose Publications, 2001).

2   For information on Stepping Stones' bereavement programmes, contact steppingstones.mail@gmail.com. Cf. 'Acorns' bereavement programmes (acorns.info@gmail.com).

We make a difference when we accept that bereaved people are trying to deal with the 'Who am I now?' question

Every loss brings with it searching questions of personal identity: for the widow or widower after many years of marriage; those who are bereaved after a short marriage, with the loss of hopes and dreams; the death of a parent bringing with it a new vulnerability; the loss of both parents (the 'orphan' issue), the ultimate in having to grow up; the death of a much-loved grandparent, uncle, sister or friend; the death of a child, or being unable to have children; the loss for grandparents of the children their offspring cannot produce; the loss of parenthood for gay people; loss of a job, a redundancy, a demotion, a failure to be promoted, a bankruptcy; loss of home or status; loss of limbs or sight; dementia, the loss of someone who is still alive, including the loss of acceptance and expressions of love for the carer. All these issues present people with many questions. But, perhaps the most profound and overwhelming is this one: 'Who am I now?'

In all losses, there is the painful struggle to understand who we are – our place in the family, in society, at work, at church. What role do we now fulfil? Why are we still here, following the cataclysmic changes loss brings? Is there any point in going on with life? In the 'new normal', who am I now? As carers who seek to make a difference, we can begin by accepting that these questions are normal in bereavement. Clarity will take time to evolve. But we can help profoundly by giving people time and space to find their own answers.[3]

We make a difference when we help people understand and learn to live with the permanency of loss

Our expectations of healthcare encourage us to push mortality away. We believe everything is treatable and fixable. Healthcare is like a 'car repair shop': every rattle has a solution; once the experts have done their job, the car will run as good as ever. Living with loss isn't like that. It can be understood and supported with patience, constancy, listening. But there is no magic wand to take it away. Loss is permanent.

We can help bereaved people live with bereavement so that life can grow round the gap the loss has created and there is the beginning of acceptance. Mostly, people learn to do that. Sometimes – years on – they'll still curse their loss. But with good folk like you and me, they'll be able to be honest, grieve as they should and find the healing and wholeness they rightly crave.

Let's be courageous and offer new ways of allowing bereaved people to feel that they are being supported. Let's be confident in believing that support, appropriately planned and delivered, can make a difference to those who are confused, uncertain and isolated in their grief.

There are many voices calling out for comfort, Lord.
Each is an individual loved by you,
in need of reassurance that you are with them
even and especially in times of struggle.
As we hear those voices now, we pray . . . ∎

life can grow round the gap the loss has created

---

3   To look at this as a spiritual issue, see Ewan Kelly, *Meaningful Funerals: Meeting the Theological and Pastoral Challenge in a Postmodern Era* (London: Mowbray, 2008).

THINK

How do we cope when the care we offer doesn't appear to 'make things better'? How do we deal with wanting to give up caring because we feel inadequate?

How easy is it for us to accept that deep feelings (e.g. anger, distress, guilt, depression) are healthy human expressions of grief? How do we validate these for those who struggle with them because they have a faith and deeply held beliefs in the comfort God offers?

What structure might we think about in our local church that would see bereavement support in the hands of the whole people of God and not just the minister?

READ

As well as the publications referenced in the footnotes, it is worth looking at:

Rebecca Abrams, *When Parents Die* (Abingdon: Routledge, 1999), on the death of parents.

Susan Wallbank, *Facing Grief: Bereavement at Ages 18–28: Bereavement and the Young Adult*, 2nd edn (Cambridge: Lutterworth Press, 1996), for teenagers.

Debi Gliori and Alan Durant, *Always and Forever* (London: Random House, 2003); Virginia Ironside, *The Huge Bag of Worries* (London: Hodder Children's Books, 2011); Susan Varley, *Badger's Parting Gift* (London: Andersen Press, 2013), for children.

ACT

Think about who might be involved with bereavement support developments. If people identified might be willing to be involved, look at what training might be appropriate or necessary.

Discuss which other local agencies might be contacted for advice, referrals or ongoing cooperation.

Look at ongoing supervision and support for those involved with any bereavement support structure. Review, change and develop what's offered depending on feedback from participants.

Lord God,
your Son Jesus
said let the children come to me.
May we enfold those children who are struggling
with the same openness and love.

Your greatest desire
is that we are reconciled to you.
Help us to build bridges
where relationships are broken.

Throughout the generations
you have gathered in those on the edges.
May we reach out to those
who feel cut off from society.

Your Son Jesus
was drawn to those in turmoil.
Help us to recognise a mind in confusion
and to share in its struggle for clarity.

You know each of us intimately.
You understand our personal story.
May we be gentle with those
who cannot comprehend past, present or future.

You promised to prepare a place for us
and to take us to be with you.
Be with those who wait for your summons
and with those faced with letting go.

The empty cross is your symbol of life everlasting.
May we hold its promise before those
who mourn what has been
to share the comfort of what will be.

Prepare us, we pray, for every situation
into which we are called
to be your hope, your hands, your heart,
through the wisdom of your Holy Spirit.

Amen.

Tina Kemp, Associate Minister of
Helensburgh Parish Church, Dumbarton